TO THE ENDS OF THE EARTH

Memories and recollections
of a Welsh Missionary
in Patagonia

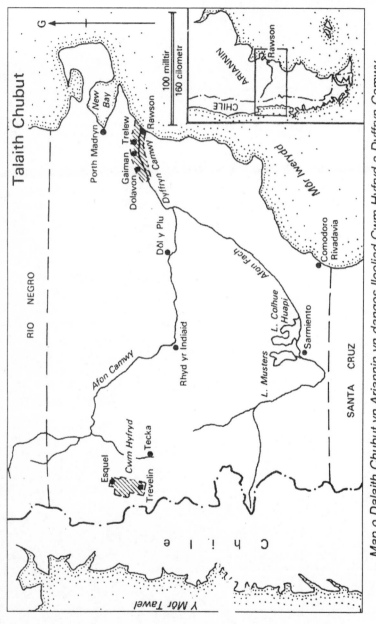

Map o Dalaith Chubut yn Ariannin yn dangos lleoliad Cwm Hyfryd a Dyffryn Camwy

TO THE ENDS OF THE EARTH

Memories and recollections
of a Welsh Missionary
in Patagonia

ELUNED MAIR DAVIES

Edited by
GWEN EMYR

Librería Cristiana
"San David"

9 de Julio 556 - Tel (0280) 4439466 - Trelew
libreriasandavid@infovia.com.ar

bwthyn
GWASG Y BWTHYN

© Gwen Emyr
Gwasg y Bwthyn
2012

ISBN 978-1-907424-37-3

This book is published with the financial support
of the Welsh Books Council.

Printed and Published by
Gwasg y Bwthyn, Caernarfon

CONTENTS

Photographs between pages 80 and 81

ACKNOWLEDGEMENTS

This book originally appeared in Welsh under the title *Hyd Eithaf y Ddaear: Atgofion Cenhades Gymraeg yn y Wladfa,* Gwasg y Bwthyn, 2010. Thanks are due to the following:

The Reverend Carwyn Arthur and his wife Alicia for organising visits to Patagonia and for their constant support and encouragement.

The Reverend Ioan Davies for giving kind permission and support on behalf of Mair Davies's family.

Rhiain M. Davies for designing the cover.

Luned Roberts de Gonzalez, Tegai Roberts, Edith MacDonald and Flavia Chaves Picón for all their assistance, and the editors of *Y Drafod* for permission to publish items which first appeared in that newspaper.

Dr Phil Ellis, Mair Eluned Davies, Catrin Roberts, Ceinwen Swann and Dr Mary Nicholas for the translation.

Gwasg y Bwthyn for their careful work throughout the publishing process and the Welsh Books Council for detailed advice.

John Emyr for sharing the journey.

PREFACE

This book presents the story of the Christian missionary Eluned Mair Davies (1935 – 2009) as told by herself. It also includes tributes to her by friends and acquaintances. Having been brought up in Banc-y-ffordd, Llandysul, where she received her schooling, she then attended university and college, and after a brief period of teaching she was called to serve as a missionary in the Welsh Settlement in Patagonia. In November 1963, when Mair was 28, she sailed on board the *Arlanza* to South America, where she spent 45 years serving as a missionary in Patagonia, until her untimely death, through illness, in Trelew on 20 August 2009.

I wish to explain how this book came to be written. In 2001, I was eager to learn more about the experiences of Christian women whose lives had been influential. When I began my research, I met Alicia Picón de Arthur, who was born and brought up in Patagonia, and who knew Mair well. As we talked, I felt that it would be valuable to ask Mair Davies about her background and her experiences on the mission field in Patagonia. I therefore sent questions to her via e-mail, and part of this interview was published in *Y Cylchgrawn Efengylaidd* (Welsh Evangelical Magazine) in March 2002.

Many of us have had the privilege of speaking to Mair Davies over the years, and listening to her talks during her visits to Wales. As a family we were acquainted with Mair, and I remember clearly the meeting in August 1963

7

in Aberystwyth, when we were able to bid her farewell before she travelled to the Welsh Settlement for the first time. I remember my sister, Sian (who was six years old at the time), presenting her with a small blue pottery jug as a personal gift. Over the years, many Christians here in Wales have supported Mair faithfully through their prayers and donations. We would hear news of the work through the prayer letters regularly sent out by her. Then, in the spring of 1974, my parents, the Rev. and Mrs J. Elwyn Davies, were given the opportunity of visiting Patagonia for six weeks, to help with the Christian ministry and work.

Alicia and I began our journey to Patagonia on 8 March 2002, travelling from London to Frankfurt and then on to Buenos Aires. During the journey we shared our hopes that we would be given an opportunity to talk to people who knew Mair and to ask them about her work and her influence on them. We were aware that by then Mair was approaching her 40th year of service in the Welsh Settlement, and that this milestone needed to be celebrated in some form or other.

At the time, Argentina was facing an economic crisis, but we were given a warm-hearted welcome and every encouragement to gather as much information as possible about Mair – or 'Miss Mair' as she was fondly known in Patagonia – and her contribution which was so greatly respected.

From her home in Trelew (her 'nest' as she used to call it), and with Mair as our guide, we travelled the length of the Chubut Valley, and visited places such as Esquel, Trevelin and the beautiful Cwm Hyfryd in the Andes. Although Mair was reluctant to respond to our interest in the story of her life, I sensed that her story was that of an exceptional life which needed to be made known to others. This feeling was confirmed by the Welsh settlers, known as the *Gwladfawyr*, who were so willing to tell us how wholeheartedly they appreciated Miss Mair's labour of love in their midst.

The 40th-year milestone was thus noted in a Welsh-language article, which also included tributes, in *Y Cylchgrawn Efengylaidd* in October 2003. Gomer Press responded positively to the suggestion that a book should be published about her, but by then Mair herself had begun the task of writing her memoirs with a view to publication in the Welsh settlement journal, *Y Drafod*.

Mair would occasionally visit Wales over the years. These visits became more frequent in later years because of the failing health of Mair's mother and her sister, Gwennie Price, who, together with her husband, John Price, had served with the Leprosy Mission in India. During some of Mair's visits to Cardiff after 2003, she shared her wish to write her biography, and was grateful for every support and encouragement. Her account of the first journey to the Welsh Settlement (accompanied by Erie James) appeared in *Y Drafod* in the summer of 2008, and the account of her first Christmas in Patagonia in the winter issue of 2008.

And so, from 2002 onwards, Mair set aside time to write. Despite her ever conscientious response to the many demands on her time, she succeeded in answering in greater detail the questions e-mailed to her back in 2001. In addition to this, in 2002, Mair sent other information via e-mail, which has also been included in this book. Also, with the help of Tegai Roberts of the Museo Regional de Gaiman, and the Rev. Carwyn and Alicia Arthur, other documents written by Mair, are included in this account.

There are two parts to the book. The first part contains

what Mair Davies herself wrote about her upbringing, the call to become a missionary, and the early years in the Welsh Settlement. In the second part, through a selection of tributes from friends and those who knew her, I have tried to give a glimpse of how Mair's work influenced the lives of those who knew her and respected her work and dedication. As will become apparent to the reader, some of the tributes were shared in March 2002 when Mair was still alive.

I wish to express my thanks for the welcome extended to me and my husband on our visit to the Welsh settlement over Christmas and the New Year 2009 – 2010. We saw at first hand how willing the *Gwladfawyr* were to share their memories with us and their deep appreciation of Mair's unceasing Christian testimony and her warm personality. And we also saw tears of *hiraeth* (longing) for one who had been so dear to them, months after her sudden departure to glory.

GWEN EMYR
Cardiff

INTRODUCTION

ELUNED MAIR DAVIES
(1935 – 2009)

Eluned Mair Davies was born in the small village of Cwm-ann, just outside Lampeter. When she was three years old her parents, Daniel and Maggie Davies, moved with their four eldest children to Pentre-cwrt, where four more children were born. Together, Gwennie, Eirwen, Mair, Janet, Ioan, Myfanwy, Hefin and Sulwen were brought up on Bercoed Ganol farm, Llandysul, in the Teifi Valley. Mair and her brothers and sisters enjoyed a full and interesting childhood on the farm, surrounded by beautiful countryside and overlooking the river which flows through the green valley below.

When Mair was asked in the spring of 2002 about early influences on her life, she talked about the local Christian people in her area who showed great kindness towards them, the ' Bercoed children', and who prayed for them. When Mair was thirteen years old, as a result of attending the Little Meeting (*Cwrdd Bach*), a children's meeting, in the village hall, under the leadership of two faithful brothers, Tom and Teifi Jones of Pentre-cwrt, she responded to the love shown towards her by the Saviour.

The call to the mission field was heard on two different occasions. The first was at the end of her first year at Aberystwyth University when she attended a conference for Christian students at Swanwick. Mair knew at the end of that conference that there was a mission field waiting for her.

Then, a few years later, when Mair was at Mount Hermon Missionary College in London, the call came to the Welsh Settlement in Patagonia, known in Welsh as *Y Wladfa*.

And so, on 23 November 1963, when she was 28 years old, Mair sailed on the Royal Mail ship the *Arlanza*. In those days travelling to far-off places was less common than today. Twenty days later, she arrived in Buenos Aires. After the Christmas holiday she was sent by the Methodist church for six months to learn Spanish at Bariloche in the Andes. From there she moved to the *Wladfa* to work with the Methodist church. When her original contract ended, having come to know the Welsh-speaking community and members of the Welsh chapels, she felt certain that she was to remain in that part of the world, to serve as a missionary.

Ten years later, her vision of opening a shop selling Bibles, Christian books and Welsh cards became a reality. And so, at the end of August 1974, a shop was opened within the splendid hall called *Dewi Sant y Cymry* (the St. David's Society) in Trelew. In 1996 another shop was opened in Comodoro Rivadavia, and when this closed because it was too far geographically, a further shop was opened in Puerto Madryn. These shops were an effective means of selling thousands of Bibles (mainly Spanish) over the years. In November 2001, Dr Juan Terranova, General Manager of the Bible Society in Argentina, travelled from Buenos Aires to Trelew in order to recognize Mair's great work in distributing God's Word throughout Patagonia by means of the St. David's Christian bookshops.

Mair, the unassuming missionary from Wales, worked

12

with heroic diligence in Patagonia for over 45 years. She chose to stay with the *Gwladfawyr* (the settlers), even during such difficult times as the 1982 Malvinas war, when the Prime minister of Britain, Margaret Thatcher, called on British citizens to leave. As this was not mandatory, Mair decided that she would stay, and if forced to leave, she was ready to become an Argentinian citizen. There can be little doubt that her instinctive decision showed clearly her total commitment to the work to which she had been called as a young woman.

As the tributes in this book show, were it not for Mair and her unwavering commitment, it is very likely that the small chapels in the Valley and the Andes would have closed their doors long ago. She used to travel on the overnight bus to Cwm Hyfryd in the Andes to lead the Welsh services in Seion chapel, Esquel, and Bethel chapel, Trevelin, visiting the lonely and those in need whilst there.

When Mair was Moderator of the Union of Free Churches in the *Wladfa*, she gave practical support to several people from Wales who wanted to help with her work in the chapels whether for a few weeks or for a period of months. She welcomed them to her home in Trelew and liaised between them and the *Gwladfawyr*. This meant that visitors would at some point be given all the help that Mair could provide to ensure that their visit was as meaningful and full as possible.

The *Gwladfawyr* were enchanted by her amiable personality, and were extremely grateful to her for her endless kindness. In her company, one could not help noticing that she would not compromise where the truth about Jesus Christ was concerned. I also noticed that she thanked Jesus for his love towards her every day. Early in the morning of each new day, she would read the Word

13

or a hymn, and would meditate and pray. Those verses and hymns gave her spiritual nourishment and were also a means of keeping in touch with her roots which lay deep in the Teifi Valley.

In my diary for Tuesday, 26 March 2002, I wrote that I had enjoyed an exceptional day in which Mair took me on a visit to the places that had been part of her mission field for so long. Among several memories, two pictures come to mind. The first is that of Mair pointing out the precious channels used to irrigate the land and bring life to the valley. Mair stopped the car and, as was her wont, made her way to the water's edge, encouraging me to follow her. Nothing pleased her more than feeling the breeze blowing in her hair, especially on a fine summer's day, standing by these life-giving channels. The second picture comes from the afternoon, when we were welcomed at the home of Henry and Eifiona Roberts, Maes Rhyddid. I was able to ask them about the Christian camps that the chapels had held on their farmland. I recorded Henry Roberts's impressions of Mair's contribution in their midst.

'Mair has been a great help to the *Wladfa* throughout the years. She has always been faithful to her Lord. We believe that such faithfulness to the Lord will be rewarded; not only is the individual rewarded, but also the society served by that individual. She has stood firm, serving her Lord for so many years here in the *Wladfa*, far from her country, and we have received so much from her and our gain has been immense.'

Mair Davies died on 20 August 2009. Her funeral service was held in Tabernacl chapel, Trelew, where she had led the Welsh Sunday School class until the end. She was buried in Gaiman cemetery on Monday 24 August, where many gathered to pay their final respects to her.

We heard about the funeral in the company of the Reverend Carwyn Arthur and his wife Alicia, in Pontypridd that evening. The weather, as the mourners approached the cemetery, had been cloudy. Speaking for the Bible Society in Bahía Blanca, Delfín Viano paid tribute to her life and work, sharing that Mair, with God's help, had been used to sell more than fifty thousand Bibles. A hymn was sung. The clouds began to clear and the mourners started to leave. How moving it was, as they turned to look back, to see above the cemetery a beautiful rainbow.

GWEN EMYR

Mair Davies remembers

1 – Early home life

I was brought up, the third of the Bercoed Ganol family of eight children, in a delightful spot near Pentre-cwrt, Llandysul, above the Teifi Valley with its attractive countryside of farms stretching far into the distant horizon, in the area known as Banc-y-ffordd.

We walked roughly two miles to the primary school in Llangeler and about three miles to chapel in Pen-y-bont, Llandysul, and travelled by bus to the grammar school there.

I enjoyed a happy childhood, as part of a large and hard-working family on the Bercoed farm. The whole family would go out into the fields where we would plant or harvest potatoes, plant cabbages for the cattle, help with the hay and corn harvest, do the milking in turn morning and evening, and teach the young calves to drink milk from a bucket. As a consequence we frequently missed the bus, which meant a very hurried walk to the school on the hill before the start of the first lesson. All this was part and parcel of the full life enjoyed by farm children. Perhaps the least attractive part of being a child in such a large family was the need to divide any delicacies between eight.

School days! I have so many pleasant memories, and if

some are not so pleasant, even they have lost their sting with the passage of time.

The earliest memory which I treasure is that of my mother and I going to the farmyard gate to say goodbye to my two older sisters as they left for school. Both were neat and happy and had had new clothes, and I, not yet aged four, was crying because I wasn't allowed to go. My mother then picked me up in her arms and carried me across the farmyard to the door of the house, comforting me with the promise that I also would have new clothes when I started school. But, oddly enough, although that great day eventually arrived, I have no recollection of how it was spent. However, I do remember asking my sister, on that first morning, whether the row of white stones that I could see on the side of the road in the distance were white hens.

It took at least half an hour to walk to school, and we had lots of fun en route as we were about fifteen children walking together. We had to make an early start. During those years, breakfast in our home was always a good helping of porridge. My poor mother would run to the house after finishing the milking to see to the porridge, and despite the occasional protest in the face of yet another porridge breakfast, it must be said that nothing slipped down the throat more easily than my mother's lovely *uwd* when we were in a hurry.

I clearly remember following the others as quickly as my little legs would carry me when, one morning, I saw a ten shilling note on the ground. What a fortunate find! When I reached the schoolyard, all out of breath, I asked my sister what I should do with it. Without hesitation, she advised me to give it to the headmaster. And that is what I did. Towards the end of the week, the owner of the ten shilling note had been identified and had left a gift for the little girl who had found the money. There then followed a talk from our worthy teacher about growing up honest and truthful – that a few honest pennies were worth more than a dishonest ten shillings. This was a memorable moment in the life of a child.

The school was a church school, and the first lesson every morning was Scripture. Without in any way belittling our Sunday school teachers, I am indebted to my school teacher at this school for giving us a thorough knowledge of interesting stories from the Old Testament. Joseph and Moses, David and Daniel were heroes in our young lives. How we enjoyed listening to her as she brought these characters to life with her special gift for storytelling. And how happy we felt when she asked us to put our little chairs in a circle around her on a Friday afternoon to spend the last lesson of the week listening to her telling a story. It did not matter at all that we had heard it before; hearing it from her for the second and third time was as enjoyable and interesting as it had been the first time. Occasionally, on a fine afternoon, we were taken for a walk along the local paths and through fields to collect wild flowers and given a nature lesson.

I was four when the Second World War broke out. There was a military camp in Henllan, not far from the school, and I vividly remember what happened one morning near to it. The older children had gone ahead and I needed to cross the road, but the soldiers' vehicles kept on passing by. So what could a little girl of six or seven do but cry? One soldier stopped his vehicle to ask me what was wrong. I said that I couldn't cross the road, and so he helped me do so. Remembering his kindness, I've often wondered if he also had a little girl whom he had left at home when he went to fight for his country.

The day came when we had to leave our beloved

teacher and move up to the headmaster's class, and what an important day that was! The entire atmosphere of the classroom seemed to be imbued with a new sense of responsibility and an awareness that we were now faced with a greater task. How could it be otherwise? For it was here that the older children prepared for the grammar school entrance exam. And yet, life was so enjoyable!

I have pleasant memories of my father bringing the horse and cart to meet us on stormy, wet afternoons. My mother would have sent some raincoats for us and we would nestle under a waterproof canvas thrown over us by our father. We had great fun on such occasions – in sharp contrast to the afternoon when we were caught in a thunderstorm that sent us running home in alarm, lightning at our heels. Before setting out in the mornings we would often ask my father, 'Is it going to rain today?' And, typical farmer that he was, his forecast was seldom wrong. The decision whether or not we took a coat hinged on my father's reply!

The day for me to leave the small school at Llangeler and attend the grammar school in Llandysul arrived far too quickly. We had to leave those two exceptional teachers that had given such firm foundations to our young lives. I was in my thirties and hundreds of miles away when I heard that my dear primary school teacher had died and that I would not see her on earth again. When I received the sad news, my heart seemed to turn over, and a lump came to my throat as I remembered childhood experiences under her tutelage, and realised that I would not be able to visit her anymore, something I had done regularly during holidays over the years.

Naturally, the atmosphere at grammar school was very different. We were now of an age when we were expected to have developed a responsible attitude towards fellow human beings and work. We had to help shoulder the burden of keeping the farm running. Consequently, many a time we missed the school bus in the morning because we had been slow in getting up to do the milking. My father used to rattle the milking buckets under our window as he went to the cowshed. We, half asleep, would imagine that we had got up, dressed and gone out, only to find ourselves, alas still in bed. It was then a race to catch the bus, but often we were too late. During those years, how my strides lengthened as I chased after the bus! With my heart pounding fast, I would arrive in class before the pupils came out of morning assembly so that we could at least start the first lesson together.

How I enjoyed looking out of the classroom window across the fields and the valley, seeing the distant hillside and, in the middle of a cluster of trees, the white-washed corner of our farmhouse. I used to imagine seeing my mother hard at work and my father busy with the horses out in the fields. Thinking of them brought a warmth to my heart and I felt challenged to do my best, for they were working hard to give us an education and opportunities that they themselves had not been given. At times, we would arrive home from school on a Monday afternoon and find poor Mother still doing the washing – for a family of ten – and all of us would then help her by performing tasks before doing our homework. On many a Saturday we would go out to the fields and help my father with whatever work was ongoing. I clearly remember the five thousand cabbage plants that my father planted annually – winter fodder for the cattle. Every one of us had to turn out and play our part. Tiredness of body and spirit overcame many of us before the last plant had been placed in the soil. Nonetheless, I would not be surprised if such farm work kept us out of a lot of mischief during those years and ensured that we made the most of our free time to do school work. At least it did not harm any of us: at school, each one of us would go on to achieve our goals.

A short while ago, I read of a little boy who used to keep pestering his elder brother to read him stories. For his part, the brother would tell the little one how glad he would be to see him start school and learn to read the stories for himself. Finally, the long-awaited day dawned, and the little boy was up and dressed far earlier than was necessary. When the bell rang at the end of the first day, the little one ran home as quickly as he could, and the first thing he did was to reach for the story book. But oh! what disappointment! He began to cry. He was not able to read after all.

The child believed so implicitly in his dream that he had not understood that there was a process that had to be followed before the dream could become a reality – a process that demanded patience and perseverance as he gradually, step by step, achieved his goal. I liked that tale, because this surely is why we spend time in school – to lay foundations, nurture patience, learn per-severance, prepare for life's future.

But now, no matter how fond the memories and pleasant the recollections, I must stop. I end with a Welsh hymn written by our Welsh teacher, Leslie Harries, and hope that the words sung by us, in Welsh, so many times have to some degree been fulfilled in the lives of many of the pupils of the School on the Hill.

O Father, grant Thy blessing
To work with Thy accord,
To find life's satisfaction
In Jesus Christ our Lord.

Teach us to grow up truthful
With hearts not bent for wrong,
Our work and daily learning
A font of holy song.

Whilst seeking through our lessons
For pearls of wisdom's hue,
Let us revere Thy Scriptures,
The source of all things true.

And on our day of leaving
The school that's on the hill,
Make us Thy willing channels
To do Thy holy will.

Leslie Harris (1905-1979)
Translated by Mair Eluned Davies

2 – Knowing Jesus Christ

If I were asked when did I come to know the Lord Jesus Christ, I would have to begin by giving thanks for the positive good influences in my early years, starting with my home.

My brothers and sisters and I will never forget how hard my parents worked to raise eight children and keep us in school until we were eighteen in order to give us the opportunity of a university education, an avenue that had been closed to them. We had a really excellent upbringing, with great emphasis being put on the important values in life. I clearly remember the occasional wet Sunday afternoon (when it was impossible for us to walk to Sunday School) when mother would read to us from a book such as *The Children's Bible*. She placed great importance on teaching us verses and psalms to recite in local *eisteddfodau*, and on 'National Sunday' held annually in Seion, the Congregational chapel. My mother's wise guidance was based on the Word of God.

I have already mentioned the influence of school days, and the sweet memories I have of Miss Bessie Jones, my first teacher in Llangeler Primary School. Looking back, I now realize how invaluable the Scripture lesson given at the start of the school day was to us. This teacher, more than anyone else, ensured that we were steeped in both Old Testament and New Testament stories.

Another influence on us was the chapel and Sunday School. My mother was brought up in Ffarmers, Caeo, and was a member of Bethel, the local Baptist Chapel. After moving to Pentre-cwrt, we attended Pen-y-bont Baptist chapel, at Llandysul. During the years of our youth, the Rev. Richard Morris and his wife provided pastoral care at this chapel. I clearly remember his down-to-earth advice to me when I went off to college in Aberystwyth: 'Don't put off till tomorrow what you can do today.'

Every Sunday morning we would walk to the ten o'clock service, accompanied one week by my mother and then by my father the following Sunday. It was quite an effort for our short legs to walk the two and a half miles and arrive in time. In the chapel house nearby lived two dear sisters, the two Miss Lloyds: Ann and Lisa. Every Sunday we would enjoy a tasty roast dinner with gravy at their table, and this enabled us to attend Sunday School at two o'clock. We would walk to Sunday School, return to have tea and then walk back for the six o'clock service. This arrangement went on for many years. The hymns taught to us in Sunday School have proved to be a significant source of strength in our spiritual life over the years.

During the summer of 1963, my last summer before leaving for Patagonia, my two brothers, Ioan and Hefin, my sister Myfanwy and I, travelled abroad. I remember vividly that one day, as we travelled by car across France, we started singing the songs we had learnt in Sunday School as children. How surprised we were to find the words coming back to us – one of us would remember one line, another the next, and we often succeeded to sing the entire song. On life's path, we have been richly blessed by the spiritual treasure these words convey.

Indeed, some months ago something happened to make me realize how important a role childhood plays with regard to memorizing words. I'm not one of those people who sing around the house, though oddly enough I enjoy singing when on my own in the car. A chorus learnt in children's meetings came back to me – an English chorus, even though the meetings were held in the Welsh language.

> God has blotted them out,
> I'm happy, glad and free.
> God has blotted them out,
> Just turn to Isaiah and see;
> Chapter forty four: twenty two and three,
> 'He's blotted them out',
> And now I can shout,
> For that means me.

I was amazed how these words came so suddenly to mind after being dormant and hidden in the folds of my mind for so many years.

Here is another example. For many years the Welsh settlers in Patagonia used to set a passage of Scripture to be memorized in preparation for the Good Friday services – an appropriate passage would be chosen for each age group and class. For years we would learn the designated passage, but of late this practice had died away, because of the time it took to learn – only to be forgotten within a month or less! However, last year, someone had the great idea of allowing the senior adult class to recite from memory any passage of eight or more verses. What a transformation! We very quickly polished up those scriptural passages known to us from an early age. Perhaps our Sunday Schools should place more emphasis on such work. But let's return to the topic at hand, early influences.

On our way to the Sunday morning service, we would usually meet dear Fred Smith as he cycled to his own chapel. He would dismount from his bike to give each of us children a pamphlet. We would eagerly look forward to receiving a different leaflet each Sunday. My sister and I used to say that we were keeping these leaflets 'until we were old enough to be missionaries', though at the time we had no personal experience of what the tracts spoke about. We read them with interest. As a rule, they began with a story followed by an application that would un-settle me somewhat. The leaflets would end either on a note of conviction, displaying an assurance I did not possess, or with a question that I could not answer to my satisfaction. I remember one Sunday when the leaflet depicted two hearts – one showing black stains, the other cleansed through the Saviour's precious blood. I hoped that my heart was also clean, but feared this was not yet true because I was aware of being untruthful, or of having quarrelled with one of my sisters. However, seeds were being sown.

I also clearly remember returning with my father from the Whit-Monday *Cymanfa* (a Welsh hymn-singing festival) and walking past the village hall. I recall saying that it was very strange that there was no place of worship in Pentre-cwrt (even now there isn't one, for that matter; if you want to attend public worship you have to go further afield). However, two brothers, Tom and Teifi Jones, decided to hold children's meetings in the village hall on Saturday afternoons during the summer holidays. They asked my father whether we could attend these meetings and my father gave his permission.

In these meetings we learnt the Tonic Sol-fa and sang

new songs. We heard Bible stories, and had to answer questions about the New Testament story told the previous Saturday. At these meetings – known as *y Cwrdd Bach* (The Little Meeting) – the gospel came alive for us children. Tom Jones presented the lesson and, by using a flannelgraph, brought the stories to life. Although about fifty children attended the session, you could have heard a pin drop as we all listened very intently. It was there, Saturday after Saturday, that we learnt of God's incomparable love for us through the story of the lost sheep, the lost coin, the prodigal son, the feeding of the five thousand, the healing of the lepers, and the terrible crucifixion on Calvary. Every week the lesson reached deeply into our tender hearts and we were exhorted to respond to this love, to acknowledge our need, to truly believe, open our hearts and invite the Saviour to take control – a step that is frequently ignored, neglected or postponed. That was true in my experience. Although the lesson made a profound impression on me week after week, I put off any decision. But one Monday night, as Gwennie and I walked home after the prayer meeting in Pen-y-bont, a car stopped and we were offered a lift. At the wheel was Tom Jones, our teacher in the children's meeting. Before dropping us off at the gate, he turned to the back seat and said to us, 'Tell me, dear girls, have you settled the question?' I was so glad that Gwennie, who was three years older than me, was there to provide an answer – for I knew that I could not give a positive reply. I wish that I had the ability today to speak as passionately and as effectively about the love of God and his eternal purposes as Tom Jones that night. Perhaps this hymn summarizes the message:

> Far before time, beyond creation's dawn,
> Before the sun and moon and stars were born,
> Salvation's way for sinners lost, undone,
> Was counselled forth by God the Three in One.

After listening, Gwennie responded, 'I don't know about you, Mair, but I'm going to accept Jesus Christ tonight.' And I agreed.

Both of us hurried home that night, and after going upstairs, Gwennie shared what our faithful teacher had told us with the younger children, and added, 'Mair and I are going to accept Jesus Christ tonight. If you want to do the same, then you must all go on your knees and tell Jesus Christ.'

I went to my parents' room to say my prayer. There, without using any special words or clever language, I thanked God for loving me so much that he gave his dear Son to suffer on Calvary in my place. I told him that I loved him because he first loved me and that I wanted him to have his place in my heart. I said that I wished to follow him without turning back. I felt relieved that I had finally taken this important step – something I had wanted to do for some time, but kept putting off. Here I was, aged thirteen, able to declare through God's grace:

> I am trusting Thee, Lord Jesus,
> Trusting only Thee;
> Trusting Thee for full salvation,
> Great and free.

Throughout our lives, all eight brothers and sisters have been thankful that we were privileged enough to have trusted in the Lord Jesus Christ as Saviour at an early age. We have been grateful to the people who explained the Way so thoroughly and clearly and who prayed, guiding us and helping us grow in the Faith. Scripture says: 'Remember now your Creator in the days of your youth', when the heart is tender and before life's important decisions have to be faced. Naturally this experience left its mark on us as a family and set us on a specific path.

After this, we continued to attend services and Sunday School in Pen-y-bont, and this is when we met another person who proved to be of great help to us in our teens – Henry Jones, Llanybydder. When older I was often amazed to think of how wise his advice was, and how faithfully he shepherded us. He would regularly share a story or an experience with us. I remember him asking us once, 'Do you know that the Bible says that there is no God?' We opened our eyes in amazement, of course. He then told us to look up Psalm 14, and we saw that it was the fool who had said in his heart that there is no God. Today I am unable to read this verse without thinking of Henry Jones who was a true and wise friend during the crucial years of our teens.

Some time later, having gone to University in Aberystwyth, I received a call asking me to go to a certain address. Upon arriving there, who should be waiting for me but dear Fred Smith whose work in distributing tracts to us as children has already been described. He had left the Llandysul area years earlier, moving to Aberdare. I was overjoyed to see him again. He asked about every member of the family, and having learnt that we had come to love the Saviour a tear ran down his cheek. The Lord had answered his prayers for the Bercoed children! He asked me whether I would do him a favour. I replied, 'With pleasure'. The request was to find his wife's resting place in the parish cemetery in Llandysul and to remove any weeds from the grave. This I did every holiday for many years.

3 – Called to the mission field

At Christian Union meetings in Aberystwyth, we often heard missionaries recounting their experiences in different parts of the world and describing the need for more workers to spread the Gospel. Every story presented us young people with a challenge. I remember thinking, more than once, that if I were sure that the Lord wanted me to do something similar, I would be willing to respond. The Lord soon tested the sincerity of my thoughts.

At the end of my first year in college I attended a conference for Christian students in Swanwick along with hundreds of others. The Rev. Hughie Jones led the morning Bible studies, taking his text from the minor prophets. When he came to the prophet Jonah, he said, 'There are cities like Nineveh throughout the world. They are waiting for you.' As I made notes, I wrote down his words, 'They are waiting for you', and was suddenly challenged to write 'for me'. The word 'you' always represents someone else, but what about me? I knew that I had come face to face with an important question that had to be answered, and this was not easy. I heard no more of the message given that morning; I was completely taken up with the challenge. What would it involve? What would be the cost? After giving these questions serious consideration, and having accepted the challenge and responded to it, I knew without a doubt that a small corner of God's great vineyard, a small or large Nineveh, was waiting for me somewhere, at some point in time. Many years were to pass by before I came to know the location of this Nineveh.

Before I speak of the call to the Welsh Settlement in Patagonia, I will take this opportunity to give a brief outline of what happened during the next few years.

Following the experience I have described above, I returned to university with new spirit. I now knew what path my life would follow, and this made college work more enjoyable. After graduating, I decided to do a year's teacher training, though I have never felt teaching to be my vocation. Eirwen, my sister, had always wanted to teach since childhood, and I thought that she would be a good teacher. We were very different from one another. She had a much more decisive personality than me. We enjoyed a close friendship when young until our paths naturally separated. But she was the teacher among us. Nevertheless, I was ready to make every effort to give teaching a go.

I spent the teacher training year at the University of Wales, Swansea, where another sister of mine, Janet, was a student. For teaching practice, I was sent to Pont-arddulais Secondary School – a pleasant enough experience apart from the last lesson on Thursday afternoons. A totally unruly class made this something of a nightmare. Apparently it was that type of class and I could hardly be expected to change the situation.

One of the precious things that came to me during that year in Pontarddulais, however, was the prayer that was sung in morning assembly:

Lead me, Lord, lead me in Thy righteousness;
    Make Thy way plain before my face.
Lead me, Lord, lead me in Thy righteousness;
    Make Thy way plain before my face.

For it is Thou, Lord, Thou, Lord, only,
    That makest me dwell in safety.
For it is Thou, Lord, Thou, Lord, only,
    That makest me dwell in safety.

I still sing this prayer and have sung it throughout the years. Hopefully many pupils also continue to sing the words.

The highlight of the week was having lunch at the Manse with the Rev. Vernon Higham and Morwen every Friday throughout my period there. As I conclude my reminiscences of Swansea and the teachers training year, another experience comes to mind. On Sunday, I usually went in the morning to a Welsh service at Gomer Baptist Chapel and to the English Baptists in Mount Pleasant in the evening. On this particular night I remember the Rev. John Savage, General Secretary of EUSA (Evangelical Union of South America) speaking about the work in South America. My interest in mission had already drawn me towards South America, though Patagonia was not yet on the agenda. In bringing the service to a close the Rev. Emrys Davies challenged the congregation, 'The Lord is asking tonight, "Who is willing to come with me to South America?" I'm inviting whoever feels that call to come forward.'

My heart began to pound as I argued with myself: 'You say that you are willing to go to South America, and yet you are not willing to go to the front of the chapel which is a thousand times nearer.' I could not sit quietly in my seat; I had to respond while Emrys Davies was still giving the invitation. Even now, I can hear the heels of my shoes clicking on the floor of the aisle as I went forward. I don't remember whether anyone spoke to me, but I will always remember how happy I felt as I walked home to Uplands that night. It was as if Jesus himself was walking with me – just Him and me, as on the road to Emmaus long ago. I cannot but add that, if we were more obedient to Him, more sensitive to His will and guidance, then we would encounter such sweet experiences far more often in our lives.

The next step was to look for a post, as I thought it wise to wait until I was older before going abroad to the mission field. A teaching post came up in Welshpool, Montgomeryshire, and yet again I found myself following Eirwen. She was a Latin teacher in Llanfair Caereinion, one of the prettiest towns in Wales in my opinion. For a whole year I shared lodgings with her in the home of Mr and Mrs Evans, Islwyn, until Eirwen got married. I then lodged with Mrs Wyn Owen in The Moorings, Welshpool, worshipping with the nearby Congregationalists. Mr Thomas served as minister there and brother D. J. Tudor was the adult Sunday School teacher. We spent delightful times in Mr and Mrs Tudor's company. Every Friday evening we used to walk a mile or so outside the village to their smallholding, Pantyglynnen, and the fellowship there was wonderful. It gives me great pleasure even now to remember this gracious couple.

At Welshpool Grammar School, I taught Scripture and Welsh as a second language. I enjoyed preparing simple lessons for O-level Scripture. The set syllabus included sections from the Old Testament Prophets and the Book of Acts in the New Testament. And there were encouraging results. Teaching Welsh to learners also helped me greatly. In fact, this was the first time I seriously studied the grammar of my mother tongue. Previous to this I wrote by ear – something sounded right or wrong. But that wasn't good enough with Welsh learners. The experience was both beneficial and satisfying; and each subsequent year was easier than the previous one.

Mid-way through the third year, I was suddenly challenged by the question, 'What has happened to that call to the mission field?' I realised that it had moved to the back of my mind, and it was time again for me to give it serious thought. A decision had to be made. I have often found it helpful when faced with an important choice, to take a step away from my present circumstances and view the matter from a new perspective. This is what happened on this occasion.

I had a college friend, Joyce Hughes, who was at that time working in the Lake District. We had shared lodgings in Swansea. I asked her whether I could spend the half-term holiday with her. She agreed. This gave me an opportunity to pray once more about what I believed to be God's call for me. As a result I realised that the call was still there, and that it was time for me to move on.

I informed Miss Rosser, the school's headmistress, that I would be leaving at the end of the school year. She was worried about me leaving without a definite job in place, but I felt at peace taking this step, certain as I was that this was the right thing for me to do. Thus this chapter in my life came to a close – three very happy years which had given me the opportunity to enjoy 'the mildness of Maldwyn'. The area had won a warm place in my heart. I was also leaving dear friends like Geraint Morgan (a Scripture teacher in Llanfyllin at that time) and his wife, Idwen; Elizabeth Jones (who married the Rev. John

Mainwaring) who always welcomed me warmly to the farm, and John Roberts who had just started teaching in Llanfyllin and who shortly was to become my brother-in-law. He and Janet spent many happy years in the area, enjoying both its beauty and the friendliness of its people.

4 – Mount Hermon College

I wanted to follow a further course that would combine both spiritual and practical training, and prepare me for work in a mission field. I didn't particularly want to pursue a theological course, even though such a course would have been excellent, assuming I had the necessary ability to complete it. During our time in college in Aberystwyth, five of us from the Christian Union attended a Missionary Conference for Students in Reading, hitch-hiking there and back without difficulty. The only thing I can remember from that conference was a young missionary woman, aged about 40, telling us girls, 'If any of you girls are thinking about going to the mission field, be prepared to go alone, as there are 15 female missionaries to every man on the mission field.' I'm sure that these words shook many of us girls, and for the first time I thought it best to prepare for the worst. Perhaps this led me to take an interest in a missionary college for women.

I knew the name of three such colleges in England, but had very little information about them. However, I did know that Mrs J. O. Fraser was Principal of Mount Hermon Missionary College in Ealing, West London. She had been present at an Inter-Varsity Christian Conference in Borth, near Aberystwyth, during my college years. I heard her speak at this conference and had read the book *Behind the Ranges: Fraser of Lisuland*

(Overseas Missionary Fellowship, 1944) describing her husband's great work in China both before and after his marriage. This led me to make enquiries about Mount Hermon College. I found what I was looking for in that college in Ealing. I underwent an interview, and this is where I spent the next two years, two very special years and possibly the happiest two years of my life. The academic requirements were not taxing for those who had attended university, but the importance placed on practical spirituality was invaluable.

There were about 50 of us there, and living with these women proved to be a rich and interesting experience. They came from Britain, Germany, Sweden and Switzerland, and they all loved the Saviour and wished to serve Him in some way. There were three of us representing south Wales – Megan Jenkins, Margaret Morgan and myself. We came from different Christian backgrounds, but the atmosphere at the college was one of warmth and unity. One of the girls, Beryl Ashurst, was thoughtful enough to write to me every Christmas throughout the years, passing on any news of the other girls.

Many students in the college did not have their family's support, and underwent their training without the backing and interest of their parents. I've been grateful throughout my life that my parents did not hinder me or oppose my decision to go so far away from home. They always respected our decisions as young adults, even if they did not always understand them. Saying goodbye was always painful for me, and it would have been ten times worse had I been going against their will. The only thing my dear mother would say was, 'When are you coming back? You've been over there long enough now.'

During my stay at Mount Hermon, I saw an advertisement in a paper published in Wales seeking 'a Welsh-speaking teacher interested in missionary work in the Welsh Settlement in Patagonia.' This really spoke to me, and after a period of praying before the Lord and waiting for Him to confirm His will, what more did I need? This assurance kept me from ever doubting where God wanted me to spend my life. I have often thought of those people in Wales, far more talented than I, who could have done the work so much better, but whatever the reason in God's plan, I was the one who heard the call.

After writing to make further enquires, I learnt that the man responsible for the advertisement was Bishop Barbieri. The Wesleyan Methodist Church of South America has bishops and Dr Barbieri was Bishop of Argentina, Uruguay and Paraguay at the time. He arranged an interview for me during his visit to London, and during the ten years that I worked for the Methodist Church in the Welsh Settlement he was like a kind father to me.

As to what I learnt in Mount Hermon, the emphasis of the teaching was very practical, as was the wise guidance given to us by Mrs Fraser and other lecturers. I have remembered this teaching throughout the years. One piece of advice often given by her during my time there was that we should take great care to safeguard our quiet time, meditating daily in the Word and having daily times of personal prayer. Without this we would lose out spiritually. This is the only way to avoid backsliding. And if I have any regrets as I look back over the years, it would be this – the times I have disregarded her wise advice. If we are too busy to give due time and attention to the Word and personal prayer, then we are simply too busy, busier than God wants us to be, and we need to change the pattern of our life.

5 – Days of empty pockets

Having taught for three years at Welshpool before attending the Missionary College in Ealing, I had saved enough money to see me through the course at Mount Hermon. By the end of the two-year course, any money in the bank had been spent. There were still four months to go before I sailed to Argentina at the end of November, and I recall distinctly how much of a challenge it was to keep my financial situation a secret from members of my family and to look only to God for an answer to my needs.

All students at the missionary college were expected to give up two weeks of their holidays to work at the college, answering the door, re-directing letters, dealing with phone calls and so on. Up to that time I had not fulfilled this requirement, so I decided to go to London to carry out these duties during the summer holidays after I had finished my course.

Whenever I travelled to London I would visit friends in Oswestry – John and Sheila Fields. During one of these visits a missionary meeting was held at their home one evening, and an offering taken for mission work. I clearly remember being challenged to give a pound towards the work, but was afraid that this would mean that I would not have enough money to travel to London by train the following day. I therefore gave a smaller amount, about half a crown. The next morning, I found an envelope by my plate on the breakfast table in which was a gift. I felt a sense of being rebuked as I thought, 'Had I given a pound in last night's offering I would have received it back this morning.'

Furthermore, one of the brethren who had attended that meeting was travelling in the direction of London and offered me a lift in his car. What happened that day was enough to encourage me to trust in God's goodness during the forthcoming four months. Indeed, it was to be an unforgettable experience. The Lord never once disappointed me! I experienced his unfailing faithfulness so many times that I could never doubt him again.

From then on, I often found myself travelling from place to place with only enough money for a single ticket, but fully confident that somehow or other the Lord would have no problem in getting me back. And so it was throughout the weeks that followed until I sailed in November 1963.

After arriving in Argentina, these exciting experiences came to an end. The Lord knew that, from then on, the Methodist Church would provide for me. However, I still remember one thing that happened to me. That year, those working for the Methodist Church in Argentina came together at a conference in Buenos Aires. By then, I was working for the Methodist Church in the Chubut Valley, and was keen to attend the conference.

During the conference week, a minister (who had been with us in the Chubut Valley) left an envelope containing a gift on my desk. I was amazed that a minister, earning a very small salary, had given me a gift. However, when I went to buy a bus ticket for the return journey to Trelew, had it not been for Pastor Lopez's kind gift, I would not have had enough money to pay for the ticket. My heavenly Father was fully aware of the situation and had provided for my need!

When visiting Wales a little while ago, something happened to remind me vividly of that time when my pockets were empty. I had been deeply moved during the testimony given by a young couple preparing to go to Romania to work with poor and destitute street children. When an offering was taken, I found that I only had small change and a ten pound note on me. When I thought of what this obedient couple were prepared to give, I felt I had to put in the ten pound note, even though I had no bank card at the time and had a week's travelling ahead of me. I felt sure that the Lord would meet my needs.

The next day I dashed off to see an old college friend before leaving, and she told me, 'I have two envelopes here for you.' The Lord wanted to give me £70 in exchange for the £10 I had given Him the previous evening.

Empty pockets can be exciting when we have such a great God guiding our lives. See Luke 25:35. To which I say, 'Amen'.

6 – The Journey to Argentina

A week before the date for sailing, 23 November 1963, my visa had not arrived. I had started filling in forms in April, six months earlier, thinking this would give plenty of time, but it was not so. For days, I had been holding on to the promises of God's Word to keep me from panicking and phoning London constantly to make enquiries. However, on the Tuesday morning, I realised that I had no time to lose and that I had to act.

The *Arlanza*, the ship I was supposed to travel on, was due to leave Tilbury port the following Saturday morning. I had a ticket but not the required visa. Therefore I decided to travel to London by train on the Thursday evening so that I would have the whole of Friday to make enquiries.

That Thursday evening still stands out in my memory. My dear parents took me by car to the railway station in Carmarthen, and my sisters Myfanwy and Sulwen kindly came also to keep me company on the journey. I remember the pain of saying goodbye on that wintry evening, but I also remember feeling quietly confident that I was being obedient to God's guidance. The next morning, I went to the Argentine Embassy in London, where my visa was taken out of a drawer and handed over to me in a completely nonchalant manner. I would have been so grateful had they informed me that it was there waiting for me.

The last night was spent at Mount Hermon, Ealing, the college that meant so much to me. The next morning we travelled by train to Tilbury, and those who had come with me were allowed on board ship to say farewell – my little sister Sulwen, who was 15 at the time, and Myfanwy who was 22. I was 28. Also there to bid farewell were John Price, my brother-in-law, who was in London at that time, and Pat Keeffe, a close friend from the missionary college.

Also sailing on the same ship was Miss Erie James, who was at that time working as a nurse in the British Hospital in Buenos Aires. Originally from the Welsh Settlement in Patagonia, she had travelled to London with a patient. I was truly grateful for her helpful and friendly company on the voyage. We also had the privilege of travelling with five missionaries who were working in Brazil. One couple had been there for 32 years, another couple were returning for the second time, and there was a young nurse going for the first time to work in an orphanage. It was lovely to have their company.

After the ship had left the docks, the passengers were gathered together for dinner and everyone, except me, was seated at the tables. I was nowhere to be found. Erie came to look for me and found me on deck – still waving, according to her account – even though we were, by then, far from land. I'm not sure about the waving, but yes, I do remember lingering to gaze at the receding shoreline, although I was not conscious at the time of any longing for my loved ones and the country that I was leaving behind. The newness of it all – the desire to get to know people and arrive, and the veil drawn by the Lord in his providence over everyone's future – made the first journey unique.

The 20 days at sea proved to be a memorable experience. It was like a huge hotel sailing on water, with all manner of facilities to meet every taste. Erie enjoyed the swimming pool, while I made much of the peace and quiet of the library where I could read and write.

The following morning the ship went through the Bay of Biscay – well known for rough seas. On the Sunday morning a service was held on board, when tables and empty chairs slid back and forth because of the strength of the waves. The safest and most comfortable thing to do in these circumstances was to take to your cabin bunk until calmer waters were reached.

The ship stayed for a few hours in Vigo in Spain, and we had the opportunity to go ashore. It was raining that particular morning and I was wearing a red raincoat. To my surprise, I noticed that nearly all the women in Vigo wore black, and I felt uncomfortably conspicuous in red. I was told that the women wore black for years as a sign of bereavement, and then tended to carry on dressing in that colour.

Lisbon was the next port. I remember being amazed by its beautiful bridge as we approached the city. We were able to go on a guided tour. The museum of ornate carriages formerly used by the royal family, was particularly memorable.

By Saturday morning we had reached Las Palmas in the Canary Islands where the weather was perfect, and the sun shone down upon us. Once again, we were able to go ashore. After that first week of sailing further and further away from the coastline of Europe, we had a week of seeing nothing but water and the occasional far-off ship crossing our path. In the third week we saw land again – this time the coastline of South America – with every day bringing us nearer to Rio de Janeiro. This must surely be one of the most beautiful cities in the world.

While the ship was still some distance from the shore, we could see something white glistening in the sun on a high rock above the city. As we approached, we assumed it was a statue. Then, drawing closer, we realised we were correct and saw that it was a statue of Christ with his arms outstretched above the city. We had two days in Rio and were able to take a tour to see the statue. Its size was stunning. People standing at its feet looked so small. The picture has remained vividly imprinted on my mind throughout the years. When we are far from the Saviour, he appears small in our sight; but as we draw nearer, he becomes greater. It is at his feet that we realise his greatness is unsurpassed. At the feet of Christ, it is us mortals who are small.

We went to the famous Copa Cabana beach with the hot summer sun above us. I remember being scared by the wild way in which the people of Rio drove. The ship then went to the port of Santos and we had an opportunity to go by bus to Sao Paulo, but it was too hot for us to enjoy the visit. I remember that the road from Santos to Sao Paulo wound through thick tropical vegetation. Then, on Saturday morning, we arrived in Montevideo and had another opportunity to go ashore. The Sunday morning, however, was the great day! We sailed up the mighty river Plate to the port of Buenos Aires with the sun shining brightly from a blue sky. I could hardly believe that, on Sunday morning, 14 December, I had finally arrived. It was so exciting.

Erie's family were waiting for her on shore. A young Norwegian missionary, Alieda Verhoeven, came on board the ship to meet me, and a minister from the Methodist Church, Pastor Carlos Sainz, who had been corresponding with me, was waiting on shore. At last, here I was standing on Argentinian soil, facing the challenge of a totally new life in so many ways. But I could hear the precious promise of God in my heart giving me confidence:

'The Lord himself goes before you and will be with you; he will never leave you nor forsake you. Do not be afraid; do not be discouraged' (Deut. 31:8). What more did I need?

7 – The first Christmas

Having arrived in Argentina it was important for me to apply for permission to live permanently in the country. This was accomplished without any problem, thanks to Miss Joyce Hill, a missionary from the United States. She whisked me from one office to the next in Buenos Aires until I obtained the necessary permission – a card document stating that I could remain in the country.

I was staying in the Methodist Church's theological college – *Facultad de Teología* – in the Flores area, and it was there, in the capital, that I spent my first Christmas with Rev. Lloyd Knox and his wife, missionaries from the United States. That Christmas they gave a royal welcome to five of us 'orphans' – a lady missionary who had recently arrived from Switzerland, three theological students and me.

We sang carols during the day, and everyone was asked to sing a verse of 'Silent Night' in his or her own language: Elizabeth in German, the students in Spanish, the missionaries in English and myself in Welsh. The *Cantico Nuevo*, the Methodist Church's new hymn book, had just been published, and it was a joy for me to see a number of Welsh hymn tunes in it as well as familiar English ones. Therefore, that Christmas afternoon, we went through most of the Welsh hymn tunes for my sake, and you can imagine the pleasure that gave me. They gave me a copy of the hymn book as a Christmas present, and I have been much blessed by the rich store of hymns it contains.

We also listened to a record of a church choir from Buenos Aires singing at a Dr Billy Graham meeting in the city the previous year, and among the hymns sung was the well-known hymn sung to the tune of 'Cwm Rhondda'. It was wonderful to hear the words and the tune. Although the carols that we sang that Christmas were the same as those I usually sang, but in a different language, what struck me most was singing them in the open air, in summer clothes. Evidently, Christmas in Argentina was a very different experience from Christmas in Wales where we would sit around a warm fire.

On one particular evening I went out to get something to eat, assuring myself that not much Spanish was needed to order a pizza and coca-cola. While I was eating, a Salvation Army brother came in and went around the tables trying to sell a magazine, but no one was showing any interest. I saw an opportunity to identify myself with his faith, and I offered him the only money that I had – a note the value of which I forget. He took it and gave the impression that he was moving on. However, I realised that unless given my change, I wouldn't be able to pay for the food. I didn't have the necessary language skills to explain my predicament. Thankfully, this fellow-labourer must have appreciated my dilemma and turned to give me the change I needed.

The day after Christmas, having spent ten days in Buenos Aires, I began the journey to Bariloche, which is situated at the foot of the Andes. Bariloche is in the province of Rio Negro, to the north of the province of Chubut where the Welsh settled. This journey took me 30 hours – from 9 o'clock on Thursday evening until 3 o'clock on Saturday afternoon – and gave me in those early days an indication of how vast the country was.

We travelled past acres of golden corn, ripe and ready to be harvested, and in one place a machine was being drawn by a team of six horses. Then, after those fertile acres in the province of Buenos Aires, we crossed mile upon mile of scrub-covered, semi-arid land, dotted by the occasional small, unassuming village of flat-roofed houses. How those people could make a living from such unfertile land was beyond my comprehension.

Opposite me on the train sat José De Luca, a theological student, who was to finish his practical year in the Methodist Church in Bariloche. Both of us travelled with a dictionary on our lap, as this was the only way we could communicate. At some point on the journey a young girl of around eight or nine years of age sat down close beside me. Her arms and face were covered with scabs, and I wondered whether the child was infested with lice. Had this happened at a later date, when I had gained more experience, I would have realised that her condition was caused by mosquitoes.

As we sat in the heat and dust of the journey, we suddenly saw through the windows of the train the snow-covered peaks of the Andes mountains, glistening in the sunshine, an exhilarating sight. Bariloche is one of the most beautiful places in Argentina, and I had read that there are three times as many people in that city and its surroundings in summer as there are in winter. I also understood that there were remarkable views to be seen there, high mountains and large lakes – the largest of them, Nahuel Huapi, being about 60 kilometres in length. Furthermore, when told that the area was called Argentina's Switzerland, I could not wait to get there. After a long journey across the province, it was a delight to see the missionary, Rev. Siegfrid Trommer, waiting for us at the station.

8 – Learning Spanish in Bariloche

And a delight it certainly was. Rev. Seigfrid Trommer and the family had come from Germany to Argentina eight years earlier. I lived with them for the first two months so that I could speak English. During the second month they went on holiday, and one thing I did during that time was make raspberry jam from the crop growing in their garden. I followed a recipe given to me by Mrs Trommer, and I found it to be an easy jam to make.

After the first two months, I was given accommodation with a family who spoke only Spanish, the Gaius family, which included parents and four cherished and kind daughters. I spent six months in Bariloche and received three lessons a week from the headmaster of the Catholic primary school. I well remember asking him after four months whether I should be speaking more of the language. He replied, 'Much more'.

Personality has much to do with learning a language. An extrovert may speak freely without worrying too much about being correct, while another person will think about every ending before venturing to open their mouth. I fell into the second category. In Spanish, the article has a feminine and masculine, as well as singular and plural, form. Every language probably has ways of tripping up learners. No one has ever learnt a language overnight. I remember sitting on a rock by the lake asking myself whether I would ever master it. I had been invited to dinner that Sunday by Edisto Tinao and Marina, a minister and his wife – who were very considerate towards me. They had also invited another minister, and conversation continued at the table after the meal, but I hardly understood a thing that was said.

At the beginning, I would go to the Sunday morning service where I could at least greet people *'¿Cómo está usted?'* How are you? Or reply *'Muy bien, gracias'*. But then someone said to me *'¿Qué tal?'*, and another person said, *'¿Cómo le va?'*, and I would look at them in surprise, totally lost. But these words and phrases were only different ways of greeting someone.

I will never forget the kindness of one person in particular, especially during those first weeks when I didn't have the vocabulary to enable me to communicate. Her name was Leonor Buchaillot. We got to know each other in the Methodist Church. She was a hairdresser, and would often invite me to her modest home where love and warmth seemed to fill every corner. It is only those who have spent time with someone where there is no common language who know, from experience, the amount of patience and effort required to communicate with a person when words mean nothing. And yet Leonor never once lost her patience with me, and I never saw frustration on her face. I will never forget her.

We met again, five years later, in New York. Then, after a further five years, we met in Dolavon when she and her husband from Rosario came on a visit to the Chubut Valley. I was sad to hear some years later that she had died of cancer, and I felt her loss deeply. I would have loved to have seen her again and tell her once more how much her friendship had meant to me at a difficult time.

I found the people of Argentina to be very kind

towards foreigners like us who were ruining their language with our strange accents. They will only laugh if your mistakes are funny. I remember such an occasion when I had gone one morning to a hair salon in Trelew. I don't recall what I was discussing with the woman who was cutting my hair, but I remember trying to use the word *'libre'* which means 'free' but I said *'liebre'*, the Spanish word for 'a hare'. Neither the hairdresser nor I could stop laughing. Despite the inevitable effort involved in language learning, I must say that I enjoyed learning such a warm and rich language.

Edisto Tinao and his wife Marina, whom I have already mentioned, helped to make my stay in Bariloche enjoyable. They were standing in during the absence of a missionary and his wife at the Baptist Church. I used to worship in the Methodist Church in the morning and with the Baptists in the evening. They were true friends of mine. They would welcome me as a guest whenever I had to stay in Buenos Aires, and other members of my family were also welcomed in their home. In the same way, they came to Wales once and stayed on the farm with my parents. They visited us in the Chubut Valley on more than one occasion, and preached in some of the chapels there.

Another delightful experience that came my way in Bariloche was the opportunity to meet and get to know Mr a Mrs Cohen and their daughter Pauline who ran an English boarding school there. This couple were responsible for English Christian summer camps in Buenos Aires for years, and many former campers would send them greetings from different parts of the world. When I last saw them a few years ago, both were failing in health. I have much admiration for the great work they carried out when in their prime, before their earthly house began to dissolve, and the challenge set by their example to work for Jesus in the day of opportunity, 'before the days of trouble'.

Two pupils from Trevelin attended the school: Charlie and Mary Green. Their aunt, Mair Griffiths, came to visit them one day, and I was really glad that she came to seek me out. As a result of this I was given the opportunity – a rarity at that time – to have a conversation in Welsh. I also remember the joy of meeting brother Euros Hughes and his wife, the first Welsh speakers I had met from the Chubut Valley, at church one Sunday. As far as I knew, there was only one Welshman living in Bariloche at that time, brother Ifano Williams.

While in Bariloche I was also privileged to meet the Rev. David Morris, a missionary from south Wales, who had been a minister in Trevelin for years and had established Ebeneser, a Spanish church, there. He graciously called on me on his way home from the capital. I remember that he took more than one photo of me, 'to send to your mother', and I appreciated his thoughtfulness. David Morris did a greater favour for me that day. Pastor Tinao and his wife had to go to Buenos Aires suddenly, and had asked me to take charge of the sisterhood meeting that afternoon. My Spanish was far from being sufficiently fluent to attempt anything ambitious. I had bought a book in Buenos Aires telling the story of Hudson Taylor, the famous missionary. I had selected a few paragraphs and had practised reading them as intelligibly as I could so that I could tell the story of this great man. But I knew it would be far better if David Morris accompanied me. He agreed immediately and the sisters enjoyed the meeting immensely. He was an interesting and effective speaker.

During my time in Bariloche, I placed special

emphasis on reading God's Word every day, and would read until it spoke to me and I was blessed. Besides, I had told myself that having fellowship with the Lord was a priority. Were I to lose that closeness to God through negligence, there was little point to my existence as I was so far from my family. He was my all in all.

Pastor Trommer used to preach in three languages: Spanish, German and, on a monthly basis, English. Once, when he was away, he asked me to take the English service in his place. I shared with the congregation how the Lord had become precious to me. When the meeting ended, one young mother, Angela, told me how much she wished she could have the same assurance. I encouraged her by saying that lack of faith was the only obstacle to receiving such assurance. She invited me to her home for a chat and I felt confident that she had discovered the simplicity of the Way, and had placed her trust in the Saviour. Soon afterwards, she and her family returned to Belgium and I lost touch with her. I was so happy when I received a letter from her a few years ago in which she said that she was visiting Argentina and that it would be lovely to meet again. She stayed with me in Trelew, and it was wonderful to hear her life's story and understand that she was connected to a missionary society in her country and that her daughter was serving the Lord.

During those months in Bariloche I longed to be given permission by Pastor Trommer to go to Trevelin and Esquel so that I could meet the Welsh people living in the Andes region. I had to wait until the fifth month for that permission. It was such a thrill to spend a weekend in *Troed yr Orsedd*, the home of the Griffiths family. I saw Eric and Alwen going to school on horseback in their white coats, the normal dress for Argentine school-children. It was a special experience for me to spend

Sunday in Bethel chapel, Trevelin, where I listened to the Rev. D. J. Peregrine (originally from the Tumble area in south Wales) preaching. I had hoped to record the sermon, the first Welsh sermon that I had heard in Patagonia. However, Mr Peregrine took hold of the microphone and grasped it in his closed hand throughout the service, so I had to put up with not having a recording of the sermon.

I was delighted when Ann Griffiths went to play her organ in *Troed yr Orsedd*, and I would join in the singing:

O blentyn y nefoedd, paham mae dy fron
Mor ofnus wrth weled gwyllt ymchwydd y don?
Mae'r dyfnder du tywyll yn rhuo, gwir yw,
Ond diogel dy fywyd, a'th Dad wrth y llyw.

O child of heaven, why tremble in fright
As you hear wild waves as dark as the night?
Though their sinister depth is close at hand,
Your life is safe at your Father's command.

These hymns were very comforting. Singing them seemed to bridge the distance between me and Wales and my loved ones there.

Soon after this visit, the six months stay came to an end, and I had my first experience of flying by aeroplane on my journey to the Chubut Valley.

9 – Early impressions and experiences in the Welsh colony

Naturally, my impressions were many and varied. At the beginning, I was filled with sheer elation. At last, after much preparation and anticipation, I had reached the Chubut Valley. I felt as light as a bird in the sky. Here I was, some seven thousand miles from Wales, able to speak Welsh, my mother tongue, and use it on a daily basis. I was grateful to God for his great kindness to me; for I knew that a huge number of missionaries were called to difficult fields of service, having to deal with complex languages and very different cultures. This feeling of joy remained with me for many days.

I was given a heartfelt welcome. The warmth of the Patagonian welcome is by now proverbial in Wales, and over the years I have experienced it many times. R. Bryn Williams, a chaired poet, who subsequently became Archdruid, had described its warmth when I visited him at the National Library of Wales in Aberystwyth the August before I left for Patagonia. He told me about the warmth of the Welsh people there and their unrivalled welcome, and indeed I was not disappointed.

At first, Pastor H. Perrin, and his wife, Carys, provided me with a home for a year. Then, in July 1965, I moved to a small building that had been adapted for use by a single person. Bishop Barbieri of Buenos Aires had provided the money to enable Pastor Perrin to get the house ready. It was situated behind Pastor Perrin's house, on land behind the Trelew Methodist Church. It had a living room, a small kitchen and a bathroom, and the church members gave me a range of useful gifts so that I could live in my 'little castle', as I called it.

At Christmas and on other holidays, I would be invited to accompany the Perrins to Carys' family home in Gaiman, where her mother, two sisters and brother lived at the time. On the afternoon I first arrived in the Valley they took me to the home of Gwyn and Gwalia Humphreys and their three daughters: Nelia, Marta and Glenda. (Their brother, John, was most probably away studying at that time.) I could not have imagined, that afternoon, what that home and family would come to mean to me in the future. During those early years, Marta was my teacher, correcting all my Spanish written work; Glenda taught me to drive, and Nelia had a special knack of turning up whenever I was in any difficulty. On the same day, if I'm not mistaken, we went to see their grandmother (Gwalia's mother), who had just had a stroke, and met Adah, Gwalia's sister, and a number of their brothers.

I visited their grandmother many times after that day, and each time I would read to her short extracts from *The Pilgrim's Progress*. I learnt that her husband, J. Ap Hughes, had been particularly blessed during the 1904–05 Revival, but I was not privileged to know him. Adah Fraser's home was a bright and delightful haven for me while she was alive, and she became to me an *enaid hoff cytûn,* a 'dear soul' with whom I had much in common.

I remember the welcome tea in Tabernacl chapel and

verses that the poet Elfed Price wrote for me. During my 40 years in Patagonia I've received many such poems.

I think that the first farm I visited was the home of the late Elias James and his wife, Erie's parents (Erie had travelled with me on board the ship). I went by bus, possibly for the first time in Patagonia. I found that whenever a driver called Rees was driving the bus, he always kept an eye on me and made sure that I got off at the right stop. Mrs James was waiting for me at a corner not far off, and I walked with her to the nearby farm. Having arrived I was shown lavish hospitality, and found myself deeply moved by the palpable silence of the place, even though the distant noise of traffic was to be heard on the main road. I had never before been aware of such silence, even though I had been brought up on a remote farm.

I also visited the grandparents, Mr and Mrs Lloyd Jones, on their farm in Dolavon. The small kitchen had an earthen floor, but I was so touched by the welcome and warmth of these dear people that tears came to my eyes. I had many mothers in the Valley in those days, just as promised by Jesus in Matthew 19:29 – 'And everyone who has left houses or brothers or sisters or father or mother . . . for my sake will receive a hundred times . . . '

At the end of 1964 I remember going with Tegai Roberts to an area called Tir Halen. The Welsh people there were so pleased to meet me because I came from *'yr Hen Wlad'* (the Old Country). I recall how they greeted me by saying *'fy ngeneth fach i'* ('my dear girl') many times, and looked at me in wonderment for having come such a long way. I also went to visit Tir Halen with Clydwen, and was enchanted by this rural area at the far end of the Valley.

On another occasion, during autumn, I remember walking two miles into the countryside to visit a woman who lived in an isolated place on her own. It was a fine afternoon and the countryside looked wonderful, with the leaves of the poplar trees changing colour into very pretty yellows. After arriving I was taken aback to see so many tomatoes on the tables as the woman busily preserved them for the winter.

Another memory of those early days is that of taking a tape recorder with me when visiting the sick and those confined to their homes, so that they could hear some Welsh hymns and also a service that my brother Hefin had recorded of my brother Ioan preaching in Pen-y-bont. I remember enjoying the sermon greatly, not having listened to the tape for a long while.

Another part of my ministry was to encourage those who were well and able to come to chapel on Sunday. I remember visiting a dear family who were not attending any church. They had been Catholics and had come into contact with the gospel in northern Argentina. I invited them to come to the chapel with me, and they came the following Sunday. After that, they said that they wanted to know more about the Bible and its contents, and so the following Sunday I spent time talking to them in their home, and I recall how happy their 11-year-old daughter was in Sunday School.

For all this joy and warmth, my struggle to master the language continued. After arriving in Trelew, I was given a class of 9 to 11-year-olds in the Sunday School, the lessons being in Spanish of course. It was very unusual to have a pupil who could speak Welsh. The Sunday School was really a Saturday morning school, and the pupils were very pleasant and sympathetic. If, for example, I was trying to find a Spanish word, one of them would always help me by providing an appropriate expression. I would prepare carefully for each lesson, and, at the same time, would learn many new words so that I would have the necessary vocabulary to teach the lesson effectively. I was very happy with the Sunday School material used at one stage, resources that had been prepared, I believe, by Mrs Fletcher Anderson when she was a missionary in Peru, prior to serving in Buenos Aires.

Across the road from the Methodist Church there was a *guarderia*, a home where children with special needs spent the day and were provided with meals. On Saturday mornings, they would also come across and join the various classes. I saw a gradual growth in the Sunday School each week, and we promised to hold a party or picnic when we reached 40 members. Several of us were involved in the work, and another 'Sunday School' was held on Saturday afternoons in Moriah chapel, which was about a mile and a half outside Trelew at that time. (By now Trelew has developed and reaches as far as the building.)

It was not unusual in the years following those initial days, to meet someone on the street and be greeted with the words: 'Señorita Mair, don't you remember me? I was one of the children who came across the road to the church on Saturday morning.' One day I met a woman on the street in Trelew who was one of those first pupils, and she said to me, 'I still remember what I learned in those Saturday morning lessons.' She has remained a faithful member of the Methodist Church throughout the years. As one of the Lord's servants has said, 'Old age is a time for enjoying the fruit of years gone by.'

I really enjoyed the Christian Summer schools held by the Methodist Church in Puerto Madryn during the first five years that I spent in Patagonia. I had my first experience of these schools during my first summer in the Valley. The leader was Mrs Marina Williams from the Bryn Crwn district. Marina was a teacher, originally from the Buenos Aires area, and she had come one year to the Chubut Valley with a group of young people to work with the Methodist Church in the Welsh chapels, and had later married a local farmer, Gerallt Williams. By the time I arrived, they had two sons, Alberto, aged four, and Waldo who was a year and a half. My responsibility that week was to look after Waldo, who was a very contented and happy child. I enjoyed my duties that year, and while I carried out these responsibilities the other teachers, who did not have the same language difficulties as me, led the activities.

The teachers were not always the same, but every year we had a happy time and were blessed. We would first of all hand out invitations to children living in the surrounding streets. We could only comfortably accommodate 40 in the summer school. Much satisfaction was derived from preparing lessons and craft work. Every day we would teach songs and give a Bible lesson. They also had memory verses, outside games and handicraft work (to be taken home by the children at the end of the week). Teachers had many amusing tales to tell about their experiences.

The Methodist Church during that period organised summer camps for the youth of the churches in Patagonia. They were usually held in Punta Alta, by Bahia Blanca, some 500 kilometres north of the Chubut Valley, in a delightful seaside location. Four of us travelled from the Valley to this camp during that first summer in Patagonia. I was asked to prepare a brief message for the time of devotion held before breakfast each morning and at the end of each day. I chose to speak on the theme of characters from the Bible. But I was struggling with the language and my worry that people would not understand me. Was I clear in explaining what I wanted to tell them? Should I have waited another year before accepting such a responsibility?

Despite all these doubts, I remember it as a very happy camp, and the young people had a great time composing funny verses for each other and singing them around the *fogón* (campfire) which was lit every evening. All four of us from the Chubut Valley were given a verse each, with an additional verse for me. At the end of the week, the campers would sign cards and write words of farewell to one another. I was surprised by the kind-hearted words I received from various campers. In addition, the chaplain, Rev. Aldo Etchegoyen, wrote to express his appreciation of my contribution to the camp and wished the Lord's blessing on my ministry in the Valley. It was a great comfort after all those negative thoughts and feelings.

Rev. Pastor H. Perrin had the oversight of two congregations, one in Trelew and the other in Puerto Madryn. During the first five years, I went regularly to Madryn. At one stage, I used to go every Saturday on the one o'clock bus, so that I could visit people and hold a meeting for eight young girls. All the meetings in Puerto Madryn at that time were held in the Meyer Hall on the sea front. This old building had apparently been a hotel at one time, and the Methodists rented the front room only. There was a door that led to empty back rooms. I used to sleep on a camp bed in the hall on the Saturday night and return to Trelew with Pastor Perrin and Carys after the Sunday morning service.

One night, I woke up suddenly, convinced that I had heard a noise in the building. I listened intently, and there it was again! It sounded like a chair being dragged slowly. I began to think that I had imagined it all and thought about going back to sleep. But then I heard it again. I leapt out of bed, put my clothes on over my nightdress, grabbed my bag and left the building quickly, locking the door behind me.

Well, what next? It was around midnight and I decided to go to Ilid and Elfed Williams' house where there was always a welcome. After listening to my story, they invited me to stay with them overnight. I was very grateful for such consideration. No light was shed on that night's mystery, and I never found out what exactly had made me believe that there was cause for alarm.

After a week's conference in Bariloche at the end of November 1965 (where I saw familiar faces and stayed with Mrs Cohn with whom problems were shared), I returned to the Valley totally refreshed. The only change made with regard to my duties was that I should spend the first week of every month in Puerto Madryn, to enable more time to be given to the work there. One or two people offered me accommodation, but I decided to stay in a part of the church building in order to have more independence. This also made it easier for people to get in touch with me, if they so wished.

Later on, after the church built its own meeting place, I was shown great kindness by another couple, Hilda and Baldomero Araña, and was warmly welcomed to their home. They, like Ilid and Elfed, attended the Methodist

Church faithfully. Another woman, whose generous hospitality I frequently enjoyed, was another faithful member, Nora Zahn, and we spent many a pleasant hour sharing in *seiat* (sharing spiritual matters) and singing our favourite hymns.

I have already mentioned my struggle in mastering the language during those early years. I also experienced an inner battle with myself because I felt that I had so much to learn, being shy and inexperienced in many ways. One of the most difficult aspects for me was to become accustomed to the manner in which the dead are buried in Argentina. Hot weather meant that the law of the land requires burial to take place within a certain period of time. A person could die during the night and be buried before sundown the next day – everything is over very, very quickly. A minister could be asked to take a funeral to be held in a few hours time. There were many times when I longed to be given a few days warning as happens in Wales.

I could count on one hand the number of funerals I had attended before going to Patagonia. Pastor Perrin would sometimes ask me for a favour. 'Anything but a funeral,' would be my reply. However, having said this, I gradually became accustomed to the task and took scores of funerals throughout the Valley during the ten years that I ministered in the Methodist Church.

I soon realised that these funerals were opportunities that put upon me the responsibility of sharing the Gospel message simply, succinctly and with clarity, and that to a group of people who were usually ready to listen because of their spiritual frame of mind. These people expected a clear message. In general, Sunday congregations in Patagonia are quite small, but on the day of a funeral, a large number of people from across an entire area can be present. I must add that neither my understanding of the Word nor my conscience allows me to place every departed soul in heaven, since the Saviour has stated clearly the conditions of entry.

The religious situation in the Valley during those early days was not clear-cut. When I first arrived in the Valley, the Methodist Church and the Union of Free Churches in the *Wladfa*, namely the Welsh Chapels, were holding discussions and trying to reach an agreement regarding possible co-operation between the chapels. But, despite committee meetings, it was not obvious how this might happen. Unfortunately, this caused ill-feeling between many, while others agreed to disagree in a peaceful manner.

I arrived in the middle of this trouble and tension, and was too new to fully grasp the situation and make any sort of positive contribution. The situation called for strong spiritual leadership, with people being encouraged to pray, so that brotherly love would thrive throughout and would witness to the gospel in the community. Sadly, the disagreement divided a community which, as far as I know, had lived harmoniously in the Valley since the establishment of the *Wladfa* a hundred years previously.

I was conscious of another battle beginning – a battle of faith. I had my work cut out to adjust. I had come from a close-knit family in which we, as brothers and sisters, relished getting together to share experiences and have a *seiat*. I remember three or four of us lying on a big bed upstairs discussing all manner of things that were of interest to us. But now, at the other side of the world and with no relatives, in whom could I confide? And with

whom could secrets be shared? With whom could I dis-
cuss a difficult church situation, and who could I ask to
pray with me for a particular circumstance? I had to
exercise patience, and believe at the same time that I
would, in time, have answers to each question. In the
meantime I had One who is greater than all, and who has
assured His people throughout the centuries, 'Do not
fear, for I am with you' (Isaiah 41:10).

> One there is, above all others,
>   Well deserves the name of Friend;
> His is love beyond a brother's,
>   Costly, free, and knows no end:
> They who once his kindness prove,
>   Find it everlasting love.
>   *John Newton*

During those early years, the Methodist Church used to
hold evangelistic crusades, and I know of faithful
members today who trace their personal faith in Christ
back to these crusades. I particularly think of Pastor
Alberto López and Cesar Bruno's visits: they were an
inspiration and a blessing. There were many others also,
both before and after, such as Carlos Sintado, Garoffalo,
not forgetting Guy Wilson from Texas.

The five years drew to a close. They had not been easy,
but the experience had been valuable. I could trace every
failure to the fact that I had not kept my eyes fixed on
Jesus but had been tempted to look at someone or
something insignificant. When the Methodist Church
annual conference, held during the fifth year, was
drawing near, Bishop Barbieri offered me the opportunity to represent Patagonia as a member of a team of
eight women from different countries in the world who

would visit the United States for a few months. I felt very inadequate, but I knew that it would be excellent experience, and I was grateful to Pastor Perrin for putting my name forward. It would mean ten days in New York, one week in Washington and another in Nashville Tennessee. I would then go from the United States back to Wales, for the first time, at the beginning of July. There was a condition attached to my trip to the United States – I had to renew my contract and return to the Valley for another five years. The possibility of not returning had not crossed my mind.

10 – Christian Books

I was nearing the end of the second period of five years
with the Methodist Church. During my last year in
Dolavon I had got stuck in a rut. Feeling that I was a
complete failure, I began to ask the Lord whether I was
being led towards another door on which I should knock.
I was certain that going back to Wales was not the
answer.

I would often dream about a Christian bookshop.
When I occasionally found such a shop, I would buy all
sorts of invaluable material. One day I mentioned the
possibility of working in a Christian bookshop to a friend,
and said that I would enjoy such work. Anita Lewis, by
now a retired teacher, was at the time a member of the
Saint David's Society in Trelew. Anita was very en-
thusiastic about the idea and was keen to speak at the
next committee meeting about the possibility of alloca-
ting a room within the hall owned by the society for such
a shop. In the meantime, I prayed that the committee's
answer would indicate the Lord's will regarding the
matter.

The response was positive, and from the very beginning the committee was very supportive. Mr Ieuan
Arnold was the President of the Society at that time, and
I am very grateful for the support given by the various
committees over a period spanning almost 25 years by
allowing it to be located within the Saint David's Hall

building, a fine hall in a central position. Indeed, the shop paid no rent for years, thanks to the generosity shown by these committees. The only disappointment was this: I had asked more than once whether I could move to a larger room on the other side of the main entrance, but someone would always offer a higher rent. However, under the presidency of Wendel Davies, the shop was extended significantly, and these improvements made the work considerably easier.

This new development of working in the shop meant that I had to leave my full-time ministry with the Methodist Church, having received kindness and companionship which has endured over the years. I now had the opportunity to offer more help to the Welsh chapels – and those opportunities increased as time went by. After all, I had come to the Welsh Settlement with that work in view.

Having felt a failure as an evangelist working on my own, one strong motivation for opening such a shop was to support the work of ministers still engaged in the battle, by providing them with good inspirational resources. I knew nothing about shopkeeping, but I had been brought up in a home where paying one's debts had always been a priority, and that emphasis would prove to be invaluable in this new venture. I had £50 in my pocket when the shop began. The exchange rate must have been good at that time. I remember fondly that the versatile missionary, Rev. Paul Williams, from the Methodist Church, made the wooden shelves. I also remember my friend Robert Owen Jones calling in to see the shop before it opened at the end of August 1974. He was about to return to Wales after spending a year in the Welsh Settlement with his family.

In January 1975 other friends, Rev. Elwyn Davies and

his wife Mair, were here for a few weeks, and we went to see a solicitor about registering the shop in the name of the Evangelical Movement of Wales. That arrangement remained in place for years until Argentine legislation made us register the shop in the name of an individual, thus making it easier to comply with increasingly complex legal requirements. Working in the shop greatly enriched my life. It was inspiring to meet Christians from different church denominations – listening to their experiences and realising that God was at work, rejoicing with them in their joy, and also sharing their sadness in difficult times.

In those early years, the various Spanish churches used to invite the shop to run a bookstall whenever conferences, crusades or family camps were held. At that time, I had plenty of energy and could happily accept such invitations, sometimes on a Saturday afternoon or evening, or a Sunday night after I had finished ministering in the chapels.

Whenever I had a free Sunday, I would invite a young woman to join me for company and we would travel south together to Comodoro Rivadavia city and visit four or five churches. I would be welcomed there with open arms and would sell many books because there wasn't a Christian bookshop in that town at the time. It worried me for a while that a city like Comodoro, with a population of about 100,000, did not have such a bookshop. However, in January 1997, a branch was opened there, and our friends Gwilym Humphreys and Elwyn Jones from Wales travelled 400 kilometres with us to see the shop and get it ready for opening. It was indeed an exciting undertaking.

From 1986 to the beginning of 1988, Dilys Roberts from Canada helped in the shop and in the chapels, but she had to return home because of health problems. I had known Dilys since her childhood in the Welsh Settlement in Patagonia, as her parents, Rev. Maldwyn Roberts and his wife Minnie, had come from Wales to minister in the Chubut Valley before going to Canada. Then, in 1988, Alicia Picón came to work in the shop. At that time my niece, Ruth Davies, was in Patagonia refreshing her Spanish, and had become friends with Alicia. I clearly remember her asking me one day, 'Why don't you ask Alicia to help you in the shop, Aunty Mair?' And that's what happened. As from that moment, Patagonian dust was not given a chance to settle or hide, not even on the highest shelves. In the wake of Alicia's arrival, her sister Graciela came to the shop, and by now a third sister, Claudia, helps when the need arises. And I mustn't forget Patricia, who does admirable work in Comodoro Rivadavia.

There are so many agreeable memories, and I shall end by mentioning one or two of them. I remember a young woman coming to the shop one day, obviously wanting to know about the way of salvation. I gave her the booklet *Dyfod yn Gristion* ('Becoming a Christian') by Emyr Roberts. The next time I saw her I asked her, 'Have you become a Christian?' 'Yes,' she replied, 'it was exactly what I was looking for.' And of course, there was much rejoicing. She came back again to the shop within a month, still rejoicing. Today she is a faithful member in a nearby Spanish church.

I remember a small, six or seven-year-old boy coming in with his father on his birthday some years ago, to buy a Bible. The father had wanted to buy a pair of trousers as a present, but the boy didn't want trousers, he wanted a Bible. The father had told the child that he wouldn't buy both items. But it made no difference – the boy wanted a Bible. He got his first Bible and was delighted as he left the shop.

Here is the testimony of a Christian, aged about sixty, who came into the shop to buy cassettes one day. When I asked him how he had come to know the Saviour, he told me his story. He described himself as the lowest of the low in Trelew. His life had consisted of drinking, fighting and attacking people with a knife. One day, whilst rummaging around the refuse dump outside town, he happened to notice an open book, with its pages blowing in the wind. He picked it up and, although he knew nothing about the Bible, he felt that he was holding something sacred, and so he kept it. He started asking questions about the contents, and this gradually led him to hear the gospel and to give his life to the Saviour. Today, despite his rough past, the effects of grace can be seen in his life: he is 'in Christ' and therefore a new creation.

I heard a striking testimony from a Christian in the shop one day. He had felt led to give a drunkard his Bible in a town to the north of the Chubut Valley. Then, about five years later, he met the man again in another town: he was giving his testimony in an open air meeting, holding that very same Bible in his hand. This brother felt that giving Bibles to people as he witnessed to them was part of his service to the Lord even though this was expensive for him at times.

'It is all a blessing, once we begin to understand,' said one brother. 'The best thing that could have happened to me,' said another.

I have often regretted not keeping a diary of my experiences in the shop.

I am grateful for the precious Word and for the freedom to read it and to offer it to others whilst the day of grace and opportunity is still with us. It is so encouraging to know that 130 Bibles were sold in July in the Trelew shop, bearing in mind the serious economic difficulties facing the Welsh Settlement at present.

I wonder whether the girls and I, one great day in the future, will be told what the Holy Spirit did through the thousands of Bibles and books sold in this shop over these twenty-eight years. I would really like to know.

(August 2002)

Afterword

If asked what advice I would give to a Christian who felt called to carry out missionary work today, I would share the advice given so often to us as students by dear Mrs J. O. Fraser during my time at the missionary college. That advice was, as I have already mentioned, that we should take great care to safeguard our quiet time, meditating daily in the Word and having daily times of personal prayer. Without this our spiritual life would suffer. This is the only way to avoid backsliding. And if there is anything that I regret as I look back over the years, it is this – the times I disregarded her wise advice. If we are too busy to give due time and attention to the Word and personal prayer, then we are too busy, busier than God wants us to be, and we need to change the pattern of our life. In my case, the solution was to seek help in the shop.

Secondly, I would emphasise the importance of being sure of God's guidance and will, and to fully believe that the Lord's will for all His children is 'good, pleasing and perfect' (Romans 12:2), that is, God's best. This conviction enables us to live happy, contented and grateful lives!

And then to realise that God is a debtor to no man, that Jesus Christ's words in Matthew 19:29 are completely true, as are all of His words: 'And everyone who has left houses or brothers or sisters or father or mother . . . for my sake will receive a hundred times . . . ' If my heart wept many a time as I left behind my mother and father, brother and sister, I grew accustomed to the pain of parting over the years, and I can testify that, long before I arrived in Argentina, the Lord had buried all *hiraeth,* all longing, in the vast ocean over which I journeyed. And on my return I would be eager to see the 'mothers', the 'fathers', the 'brothers' and the 'sisters' that the Lord had given me in Patagonia, a great many of whom have so enriched my life over the years. My life would have been so much poorer had I never met them and had I not responded to the Call.

> Tell of His wonderful faithfulness,
> And sound His power abroad;
> Sing the sweet promise of His grace,
> And the performing God.
> *Isaac Watts*

Tributes

The Perrin Family's tribute
(Herbert, Carys and Caren Perrin)

Here is the tribute of Herbert Perrin to
Mair Davies in August 2006.

Our desire is to unite in expressing our appreciation of
the life and ministry of Mair Davies in the Chubut Valley.

As a family, we had the privilege of welcoming Mair to
the Valley when she came to work in the Evangelical
Methodist Argentinian Church in Dolavon. She shared
our home for a while, and then later moved to a flat
owned by the church, so that she could have greater
freedom and independence.

After arriving in the country, while she was learning
Spanish for a period in Bariloche, she came to know my
parents who were pastoring there for a few months, and
we were lodging in the same home as Mair, with a family
from the church. Indeed, they were her closest com-
panions from the outset as they were her nearest links,
apart from her female Spanish teacher. I remember them
sharing recipes, as well as having meals together, and my
father teasing her on more than one occasion.

I remember another time when my father was very ill,
and we were having to travel to Córdoba, Mair travelling
with us in the Citroen. My daughter was only a year old.

And because the journey was long, we took it in turns to drive to avoid having to stop. About two to three days after arriving at our destination, and my father being quite lucid in his mind, we shared Holy Communion with him. Shortly after that, my father died and went into the Lord's presence. And to this day, one of my sisters remembers Mair being with her, comforting her with words full of compassion.

At the commencement of her ministry, Mair had to take part in a project in Christian Education with children and young people, and she also participated in activities with women. In those days she used to say that she was unable to 'preach'. However, preaching has been one of her strengths throughout the years of her ministry in the various Valley chapels.

Without doubt, she was kept by the grace of God, strengthened by the Holy Spirit, to bring comfort and hope in Christ to those in need.

A story

Mair had been in the Valley about five years when she received an invitation, because of her work amongst the women, to go to an event in the United States of America. Representatives from the four corners of the globe would be present in the gathering.

As the churches of the United States were funding the trip, she considered the possibility of including Wales in a triangular journey, knowing the cost would be exactly the same. The aeroplane was departing from Ezeiza on 28 February – the date of her birthday. I used to enjoy amusing Mair by paying the occasional light-hearted trick on her. On this occasion, what I prepared was a heartfelt message. I wrote a letter on official church newspaper to the captain of the aeroplane, saying that she had left her family in Wales, dedicating years of her life to serve us. Could he, as a token of thanks, greet her on her birthday? The letter was sent by the hand of Héctor Garciá Guillén (the husband of Gloria Hughes), who was working in Trelew airport.

Early in the journey, a member of the crew asked her if she was Mair Davies. Then he came with a tray with champagne on it and wished her a happy birthday. The other passengers were glad to have the opportunity to join in the good wishes, and another member of the crew gave Mair headphones, so that she could listen to a song specifically chosen for her.

When Mair asked how they knew that her birthday was on that date, she was told, 'The Pastor from Trelew told us.' We heard later that Mair raised her hands and said in astonishment, 'Pastor – you've come with me even here!'

(August 2006)

Bercoed Ganol, side view

The eight children outside Bercoed Ganol farm, Llandysul.
(Back row from left to right: Janet, Eirwen, Mair, Sulwen on Gwennie's
lap. Front row: Hefin, Myfanwy and Ioan)

Y Cwrdd Bach (The Little Meeting) in Pentre-cwrt, 1949.
(Mair is fourth from the right in the second row from the back)

Mair and her mother at a family wedding in the 1970s

Mair with her parents – Daniel and Maggie Davies

Mair in the company of friends in the garden of Carpenter Hall,
Aberystwyth, June 1955:
Eirwen   Ceinwen   Magwen
Mair   Elina   Eunice

College days.
(From left to right: Eirwen, Magwen, Mair, Ceinwen, Eunice)

Mair on board of the
Arlanza, with Erie
James from Gaiman,
in November 1963

Mair in Bariloche, 1964
Photo: Rev. David Morris

Mair with members of the Methodist Church, in the early days.
(Mair is the third from the right in the front row)

The Centenary Eisteddfod – 1965.
(Mair on the left. Dafydd Wigley in the front row)

Mair in the company of Gwalia and the three daughters

Mair with Carys Perrin in front of the Methodist church in Trelew during her early days in the Chubut Valley

Mair near Esquel, the Andes, at the start of her return journey to the Chubut Valley in her Renault 4 (1992)

Dr Phil Ellis and his wife, Angharad, shortly before their year of service in the *Wladfa*, 1987–8. In the words of Mair Davies, in 2002, 'We often remember with warmth and gratitude Dr Phil Ellis and his wife Angharad's visit to the *Wladfa*, and Phil's effort to organise the first summer camp for the young people of the Welsh chapels in the *Wladfa* – Phil, who was fluent in Spanish, was leader and chaplain. The subsequent challenge was to persevere every year; we are grateful that the Lord has enabled us to fulfil the dream. By today, several of our Sunday School teachers are the result of the camps.'

The Sunday School Class in Tabernacl, Trelew, in 1994, on the occasion of celebrating Mair's 30 years of service in the Chubut Valley.

(In the front row, Elena Arnold on the left, and Mair on the right)

Mair in the company of Elena Arnold

Mair with her sister Gwennie Price,
at Bercoed Ganol, July 2003

Outside St David's Christian Bookshop in Trelew

An article about the Christian Bookshop in Trelew
published in the Argentinian Christian newspaper,
El Puente (The Bridge) in the summer of 1990

The Christian Bookshop in Comodoro Rivadavia
which was opened in 1996

Graciela and Alicia, in January 2010, outside the Christian Bookshop
which is run by Graciela and her husband, Javier Sapochnik

Carwyn and Alicia Picón de Arthur on their wedding day in August 1999

Mair in the company of Carwyn and Alicia in the summer of 2000

Christmas with Alicia Picón de Arthur's family

Mair, Gwen Emyr and Graciela bidding farwell in
Trelew airport, March 2002. *Picture: Alicia Arthur*

Unveiling a slate plaque from Wales during the centenary
of Bethesda chapel (2004)

The first retreat for members of the Welsh chapels.
In the Bible College, Bryn Gwyn. February 2005.
Leaders – Pastor Lorenzo Strout and his wife Melissa, missionaries from the USA

Celebrating Mair's 70th birthday on 28 February 2005.
The party was held in the new hall in Tabernacl, Trelew

Mair, Gerallt Williams, Ada Lloyd Jones de Garavano,
Eileen James de Jones and Ilyd Lloyd Jones de Williams
outside Glan Alaw chapel (13 March 2005)

Mair and Alieda Verhoeven's reunion in Mendoza
in April 2005. They met initially in December 1963
when Mair arrived for the first time in Buenos Aires

Mair outside Bethesda chapel during the visit of her sister Janet and her husband John Roberts, in 1998

A day's retreat, September 2005, in the company of friends.
Olivia Brooks, Elena Arnold, May Hughes, Ines Mellado, Almed Thomas
and Mair Davies

Mair sitting by a typical water channel in the Chubut Valley

In Alicia and Carwyn's garden in Pontypridd.
Photo: Alicia Arthur

In the kitchen of Henry Roberts's farm during Mair's
last summer camp (January 2009). Virma Griffiths de Hudson,
Albina Real de Mulhall, Mauricio Mulhall, Tegai Roberts and Mair.
Photo: Tony Poole

Singing festival in Nasareth, Drofa Dulog, with Edith MacDonald by the window and Rebeca White conducting (20 June 2009).
Photo: Raul Horacio Comes

Mair speaking at *Gŵyl y Glaniad* (the Festival of the First Landing), Moriah Chapel (28 July 2009).
Photo: Raul Horacio Comes

Carlos Ruiz and his wife Marcela.
Carlos is Mair's successor in the work through the
medium of Spanish in the Chubut Valley.
Photo: John Emyr

Mair in our midst
by Gweneira Davies de Quevedo

Gweneira Davies is a familiar name to readers of the annual National Eisteddfod's publication of compositions and adjudications, having several times won the competition for those residing in the *Wladfa*.
On 1 December 2009, Gweneira was honoured, by the nursery school of Playa Union, near the city of Rawson. The new nursery school was named after her: 'El Jardin de Gweneira' ('Gweneira's Garden').

I cannot but share some thoughts about the beloved missionary who ministered amongst us for over forty years. Over four months after her death, I now feel her loss even more than I could have forseen. I might say that our feeling is that of orphaned children who remember one who supported us ungrudgingly at all times.

I refer to Miss Mair Davies, '*Y Wladfa*', as her friends in Wales referred to her. In fact we considered her as one of ourselves in the Settlement and there was great respect for her not only amongst the Welsh people but also amongst indigenous people, great and small. Many local residents turned into the Christian Bookshop that she established, initially in a little corner of St. David's Hall. Then, as the shop grew in line with demand, she rented two more suitable rooms in the centre of the town, so that readers could choose their message in books or religious cards in greater comfort.

As the shop developed, Mair took a little girl from a humble, large and welcoming indigenous family, to help her. She came to know this ten-year-old girl from the little village of José de San Martin at the foot of the

Andes – who came to serve as a maid in Trelew, during her school holidays – when Mair was on one of her frequent missionary visits around the town. Her name is Alicia, and she is one of the young girls to whom Mair gave the advantage of further education by supporting her in every possible way in her studies and in her tuition, in order to learn the Welsh language.

Alicia was encouraged to attend a Welsh class, and then travel to Wales to pursue a course, as did many young people who succeeded in improving their proficiency in the Welsh language.

It could indeed be said that Mair adopted Alicia, and, while she was in Wales, Mair welcomed Alicia's sister, Graciela, to assist her in the shop. Once again she nurtured her in the faith until she became a gentle teacher able to teach a class of children in the Sunday School in the Spanish sector, and she also led many meetings at Tabernacl chapel. Graciela is now married. With her husband, Javier, she continues to look after the Bookshop, and that in a fitting manner and with considerable success.

Alicia, for the last ten years, has been married to the Reverend Carwyn Arthur, who came to the *Wladfa* for two years in October 2003, to minister in a number of chapels in the Valley. They now live in Wales, and she has made her home there for several years, working alongside the Reverend Carwyn Arthur.

As I see it, Mair had a happy time in our company, and when I asked her once when she returned from Wales, 'Is your heart divided now perhaps, Mair?' she answered that her home was here as well as over in the land of her birth.

She would often recall her first impression of the Christian life in the *Wladfa*. When she went to preach the message, she saw a host of ladies in their best hats, singing in clear voices and striking up the familiar hymns. Everyone appeared confident and happy and extended a welcome to her at all times. She felt herself comfortable in every concert and home that welcomed her.

Mair's presence as well as her faithfulness drew us to her in every situation. Her even temper, gentle voice and faith reinforced our strength and faith also. Mair's car was always full when she needed to carry others to a meeting or a funeral. Always accommodating, she gave of her time to go to families suffering from worry, sickness or trouble, and she was always willing to contribute to any good cause.

She greatly enjoyed the company of members of her family who came over, and everyone from Wales who met her. Indeed she was very talented, but, graced with practical humility, she did not make an exhibition of her talents. I was much taken with the charming verses she wrote for a literary meeting on the subject 'Home'. I was so entranced by these simple descriptive verses that I learned them by heart. *(see page 123)*

Mair came to see me two days before she became ill, as I had experienced a fall that forced me to rest for a long time. She was happy as always, and spoke of the visit of the Reverend Tegid Roberts and his wife Nant who were coming to stay in the *Wladfa* for a year, and also of the visit of Professor Robert Owen Jones for a period of three months, according to his custom as an examiner of the Welsh classes. She was looking forward to greeting them, but unfortunately she did not have the privilege of meeting and introducing them as she had expected.

I had a phone call informing me that Mair was in hospital and that her condition was rapidly deteriorating. The doctors did not have time to complete their test investigations. It is hard to believe that she has left us so suddenly, and we cannot imagine that we shall not see her again in the course of our everyday lives.

Since she was always confident that the door of heaven was open to her, may she know peace in the arms of the Heavenly Father whom she loved so faithfully with all her heart throughout her life. Yes, I have *hiraeth* or longing for Mair who greeted me so cheerfully and was always ready to help me choose the right word in my writing, if I had any misgivings. So, I pay her this tribute, being very thankful for her presence in our midst for so long.

(January 2010)

Valmai and Derlwyn Thomas, Gaiman

Derlwyn Thomas died at the beginning of
December 2009.

We as a family think the world of Mair and know well her hard work and faithfulness. She is a very dear person.

She was a Sunday school teacher to Gladys and Glori (who currently lives in Waunfawr, near Caernarfon with her husband John Roberts). Our other daughter, Glenda, worked with Mair in the camps and in the work with the young people. Through Mair's work amongst us, the three girls have been kept from many harmful influences. Our gratitude to the Lord is great.

(March 2002)

The memories of Albina Pugh de del Prado, Rawson

Josiah Williams of Carmel, Treherbert, Glamorgan, came to the *Wladfa* in 1875. Albina's mother was descended from him. The family Bible is on the dining table, although by now Albina, because of partial blindness, is unable to read it.

After losing Mair, I feel bereft. She was here ten days before she died, sitting right there talking to me. She was never one to waste a minute, but she had come specially to see me and ensure that I was well. She was indeed a true friend.

When Mair came into our midst, aged 28, I lived on the farm and did not go to chapel. I remember I was a long time before becoming a Christian. I wasn't in earnest, not zealous. But Mair would call sometimes to ask if I would teach the children to sing, and I would always agree – I could never refuse.

When I left the farm, as it became too much for me over thirty years ago, I moved to Trelew to live. There I began to go to Tabernacl chapel in the evening. I am very fond of singing. I would sing and listen to the sermon. One afternoon, when we were talking as a group outside the chapel door, Mair asked, 'You don't come to Sunday School, Albina?' And I replied that I went in the evening to hear the sermon.

'Oh, you're a one-meeting-person,' Mair said.

I felt such shame, mind, that I remember the experience to this day. To think someone could be carefully taught to do something, in one's childhood, and then stop. As long as one is able, one should do one's best, and indeed I have enjoyed Sunday School very much ever since. I would undertake the work when Mair was away, and would be blessed, that's the only word for it. By learning to share with the class, I would benefit to a greater degree.

Mair, therefore, brought me back to Christian work. It is easy to say 'I believe', and then stay at home. Mair reminded me of this: 'When you receive Jesus, speak about Him.' And do you know, I believe that from the bottom of my heart. Sometimes, as one speaks about Jesus Christ, one receives a hostile response and people can be hard in their opposition to us, but on other occasions we won't be the worse for speaking.

Mair was a great one for encouraging others to take part and praying publicly in services. So I began to help Mair in the small chapels of the Valley. Mair would ask me whether I would sing a hymn in the service, and I would agree to help the meeting on its way. I, for my part, thoroughly enjoyed contributing. I shall sing as long as I live, you can be sure, because we were taught from a very young age to sing, read music and conduct.

Without doubt, Mair had a gift for empathizing and showing concern. Well, I think she was my very best friend, as she indeed was a friend of many years standing. I knew everything about her and she knew me likewise. I would say to her it was only fair that she be allowed to go over to see her family, and this is how Mair would answer (around the 1980s): 'I like going over to see them in Wales but I would also be quite taken aback if someone told me I could not return.' And indeed, when Mair returned to the *Wladfa* the last time, a little over a year ago, she said: 'I don't know how they manage to live in Wales without the sun. There is no sun in Wales as there is here.' She emphasised that point.

When visiting us at Rawson, Mair would come for a

little break and stay with me. Later, she would come with me to hear Pastor Puyol, who is an outstanding pastor to us here, and Mair would listen to him willingly to learn from him. She never stopped learning, and that said much about her.

The people of the Valley became Mair's family. This was also true of the Andes. She spoke of little Ali as of a great treasure, and her family became a family to Mair as well. Not that Mair came here merely to pass the time, but to work and give, getting alongside everyone, no matter what the colour of their skin, their way of life or anything else.

She urged us to work, and she believed in the value of work, and that is exactly what she did till her last days. Mair had been visiting brothers and sisters in difficulty the week before she passed away. One has to wonder. On the very day she visited me here, she had been to see Blodwen Evans, who is, I believe, 92 years old, in hospital, and has since recovered. Such a one was Mair.

(27 December 2009)

Tegai Roberts, Plas y Graig, Gaiman

Tegai Roberts and her sister Luned are descendants of Lewis Jones, one of the founders of the Welsh Settlement. Tegai is the Curator of the Museum in Gaiman and Luned was the head teacher of Camwy College, Gaiman's secondary school, and a skillful leader in the Valley. One of the responsibilities of these two sisters is to run the weekly radio programme in Welsh and Spanish.

I have known Mair from the outset, and we have been very close to each other.

I consider Mair one of my foremost friends, if not my best friend. She was a very genuine person and one with whom I could share things that I would not share with any other, even my own sister. You could be sure she would keep any confidences completely secret.

Mair worked with tenacity and quietness over the years, and without her work many chapels would have closed. Her effort has kept the little chapels of the Valley open. She used to go every Sunday to these little chapels: for example, Berwyn in Rawson, Carmel in Dolavon, Bethesda and Bryn Crwn, Bryn Gwyn and Drofa Dulog, to name only a few, and she would strive to maintain services regularly. One preacher came from Wales, and his advice to her was not to waste time on small chapels and to focus on the chapels in the towns. Thankfully Mair ignored his advice. Had she agreed, there would be no small chapels open today.

From the point of view of content, Mair's preaching was good and sincere always. Also, her sermons were very relevant. I remember one sermon on giving – not a popular theme. My sister thought she should preach that sermon again.

We always looked forward to hearing Mair, and what we as listeners will miss most, now that she is departed, will be her presence and her preaching. We often thought how privileged we were to have Mair. She would preach for a little over twenty minutes, and we never felt it was too much because she had a word for our souls. She often referred to the hymns and heritage that are ours.

As to her character, Mair was unassuming and gifted. She was a mainstay and support in everything, and for a while she gave Welsh lessons. Many old books were thrown away or burnt, I daresay, but Mair would preserve many valuable books in the back of the shop. In a word, she was always ready to shoulder her responsibility.

She could write and compose poetry, and the poem that comes to mind is the one she wrote on the centenary of Moriah Chapel, Trelew. (*see page 125*)

Mair was very busy before her sudden demise. She was present at an infant dedication service in Tabernacl chapel, Trelew, in the morning, and in Bryn Crwn chapel, Bethesda, in the afternoon, where she was asked to conclude the service in prayer. In the evening, there was a communion service in Gaiman Chapel, after which she went to a see an exhibition of pictures by Juan Carlos Segura. She called to see us later, in Plas y Graig, and had a cup of tea and a light meal, as was her custom, before a meeting in the Evangelical Church in Belgrano Street (Mission) at eight o'clock. A missionary by the name of De la Llave had come from Buenos Aires to preach, and she asked me whether I would like to go to listen to him. I had not intended to go, but I went, as company to Mair, and it was worth going.

89

The following day, that is Monday, she went to Puerto Madryn, and she called on her journey, to see the family that is now helping Ilma (who is an invalid), to invite them to go to the meeting in New Gaiman on the Tuesday evening, so that they too might hear the missionary from Buenos Aires. That was typical of her.

After a night in Puerto Madryn with her friend Ada and her husband, she returned on the Tuesday and came here to the meeting in New Gaiman in the evening. She had tea with Eifiona and then she took the opportunity to see William Henry Roberts, who was frail and unable to get out of bed. The following morning Mair became ill.

Luned Roberts de Gonzales, Plas y Graig, Gaiman

Mair had somehow always been here, working hard in the chapels. Unlike many people who were full of flashes of fire, Mair persevered.

Consistency characterised her, and that in a wide range of work – preaching three times on a Sunday, travelling the length and breadth of the Valley, teaching in Sunday Schools, leading the week meetings, and for years she ran the shop that sold Christian books in Trelew. The work of the shop is far wider in its scope than the work in the chapels because there she reached all kinds of people, providing an invaluable service to the community. There Bibles are available together with all kind of books at reasonable prices, to help people improve their knowledge.

Mair has left us much sooner than we had thought. We feel a great loss, as her contribution was so important.

Within the Union of Free Churches, Mair was steadfast in her principles. She was black and white, no tossing and turning. She was adamant that the people who preached in the Welsh chapels should be those with principles. Mair prayed a great deal, and came to Edith MacDonald's home every week to a prayer meeting. This she greatly appreciated. Her prayers were like sermons.

Her sermons were Scriptural at all times, and her Welsh was so rich. Although she had learned Spanish, she never lost her Welsh. And her Spanish, indeed, was excellent. The only problem she had was the subjunctive. When preachers came who could preach in Spanish, she decided to preach solely in Welsh.

Speaking at the Festival of the Landing (*Gŵyl y Glaniad*), she urged everyone to attend chapel, and to exercise faith. Towards the end she made an appeal for people to remain faithful to the Welsh language, and said that the only way to keep the language alive was to speak it. Therefore, her appeal was 'Speak Welsh with one another'. I was sitting in quite a prominent position and found it difficult to take notes. I told her after the meeting that I was eager to publish her words in the *Drafod*, but she died shortly afterwards.

Mair thought much about the future of young people. Camps were very important to her. At the same time, she did not forget the older people, those disabled like Ilma, for example, and losing Mair has been a great blow to her and many others unknown to us.

Take, for example, Carmel Chapel, in Dolavon: the only meeting they had as members was the one led by Mair. Therefore, during the week before the service, Mair would faithfully go around the farms to inform the members that the service would be held that Sunday.

But Mair also had a sense of humour and plenty of it,

and a great sense of fun. She would come here on the first Sunday of the month after the evening service for a cup of tea. Bread, butter and jam was her choice of supper, and the three of us would be found chatting about everything. That was our way of relaxing. Sometimes she would ask to borrow something light to read, and I would lend her the latest books I had read, and she greatly enjoyed them, for example, *The First Lady Detective Agency*, which is excellent.

Another thing we have lost with Mair's death is the connection with Wales. She was so involved with the Evangelical Movement, *Y Cylchgrawn Efengylaidd*, and the calendars, but who now will maintain that link? There it is, that's how life changes, and so we are thankful for the years of faithful and uncomplaining service that Mair has given, and the great privilege we have had in knowing her.

(2 January 2010)

Edith MacDonald, Gaiman

Edith is a former teacher at the Music School and a conductor of choirs, including famous congregational choirs. She has visited Wales several times and collaborates effectively with her brother, Elvey MacDonald, who acts as a bridge between the *Wladfa* and Wales.

Mair loved the *Wladfa*. A week before she died, I asked her where she would now like to live. And do you know what her answer was? 'Do you think I could live without the sun of Patagonia? If I should die, I would now like to be buried in the cemetery here in Gaiman.' And that's what happened a little over a week later.

I remember Mair when she first came to work in the *Wladfa* with the Methodist church back in 1964. We lived in the stone house across the road here in Gaiman, and she would join us as a family to sing many hymns.

Then, when the churches in the *Wladfa* split, Mair decided to meet the need in the Welsh churches, because she had worked with the Welsh. Years passed without us seeing one another as often, as our family chose to stay in the Methodist Church. Then, in 2003, a nephew of mine learned that he had cancer. Carwyn Arthur came here to ask if he might read and pray with us. I was happy to agree. Then Mair began to come every week and she continued to visit each week from then on. Tuesday was our day at first, and then Thursday.

There is such a gap in the Valley after Mair's departure, a gap no one, in my opinion, can succeed in filling. Her faithfulness and loyalty made her a true friend. She knew how important it was to keep a confidence, and as a result I could trust her entirely, and enjoy an hour to an hour and a half reading hymns, singing and praying. Mair's way was very endearing to everyone, visiting and praying for all those known to her and in need.

She was also a very honest person and very evangelical. It was a great concern to her that people might leave this world without Jesus Christ. And from the standpoint of her belief, she was very Biblical and no one could dissuade her. In her sermon at the Festival of the Landing in Moriah last August, a little over three weeks before she left us, she urged those present to come to Jesus Christ, and pressed those Welsh who were present to come to chapel to hear more. The last sermon I was to hear from her was inspiring indeed.

She evangelized, not only with words but by her whole way of living. I can't help thinking of what the Scriptures say about Christians being like Christ's letters. Mair knew well what it was to suffer abuse for the Gospel, yet, when she was praying, her face would be transformed because she had fallen in love with Jesus Christ. She knew from experience that he was the one who would guide her in every circumstance. She emulated her Saviour, who was not ashamed to wash the feet of his disciples, and she sought to uplift her Saviour in everything that she did.

She realised, as I did, that the Welsh language opened doors – for example, to the riches contained in Welsh hymns, and she was glad to see more committing themselves to learning the language in recent years. We think of the richness of these words:

Dyma gariad, pwy a'i traetha?
  Anchwiliadwy ydyw ef;
Dyma gariad, i'w ddyfnderoedd
  Byth ni threiddia nef y nef;
Dyma gariad gwyd fy enaid
  Uwch holl bethau gwael y llawr;
Dyma gariad wna im ganu
  Yn y bythol wynfyd mawr.

Wondrous love! Who may express it?
  Indescribable indeed,
Wondrous love! Its depths to fathom
  Heaven itself could ne'er succeed.
By that love my soul is lifted
  Out of every earthly care;
Wondrous love! I'll sing its praises
  In the eternal land so fair.
                    (Mary Owen 1796–1875)

This is the hymn that comes to mind now on a summer's eve, as we converse and remember Mair.

Over the years, Alicia's family became her family. She had adopted Alicia as a daughter to all intents and purposes, and she thought the world of Carwyn, and remembered and prayed for him in his work.

· · ·

In her last moments, it was obvious that she was speaking to God. When the doctor asked her how she was, the Spanish words Mair spoke were:

  Señor, me encomiendo en tus manos,
  me encomiendo en tus manos.
  Qué lindo! Qué lindo!
  Qué hermoso! Qué hermoso!

(God, I place myself in your hands,
I place myself in your hands.
How wonderful! How wonderful!
How beautiful! How beautiful!)

(2 January 2010)

Iola Evans, Trelew

Iola is one of the decendants of Dalar Evans,
one of the early settlers who made his home in
Cwm Hyfryd. Her mother was Aaron Jenkins's
daughter – 'the first martyr of the *Wladfa*'.
Iola has therefore been born and bred in the
Andes, and she remembers her mother taking
Mair to see the lakes after she had arrived in
Bariloche.

I must emphasise how young Mair was in spirit and how
kind she had been to so many of us over the years. Indeed
I regarded her as one of my best friends. I cannot thank
Mair enough for her willingness to visit a relative of
mine, Ilma, who has been an invalid for many years. Her
late husband, Stifin, was my cousin, and Mair was their
socorro (help, aid), who fended for their needs through
sickness and very difficult circumstances.

Mair came to give us the Gospel. She lived in a way
that made people around her happy. She did not come to
teach us the Welsh language, as is the emphasis today.
Yet, she had kept her language well. And she also made
excellent use of the Spanish language in order to share
the Good News.

Lastly, I always felt that a conversation with Mair was
a constructive experience. It will be very strange without
her.

(5 January 2010)

96

Ilma Roberts, Gaiman

She was 'Miss Mair' to us. Her company, her help – everything about her was very sweet. Every week we would have a time of prayer.

She shared her company, help and comfort with me, ever since I knew her.

Indeed, it was through Mair I came to know the Lord. I used to go to chapel but I didn't understand the Gospel. Since I was six years old, I have suffered from ill-health and great affliction has come my way. I was sent to the British Hospital in Buenos Aires to have countless operations, and this led to great bitterness. I had lost all desire to go to chapel because God did not listen to my prayers. Then Mair urged me to go to chapel with her, and would give me a ride in her car. That is how I came to hear the Gospel. Then, as I began to enjoy the Sunday School and the meetings in the various churches, I would have difficulty not to cry. I bought my first Spanish Bible from Mair.

At one time, when my husband Stifin began to drink, Mair would go searching for him in the public houses, because she knew how distressed I was. Mair was tireless in her quiet diligence and nothing was too much trouble for her.

Mair, in my experience, was a very level-headed person. I feel I have a right to say this as I knew her for over 40 years. Mair had become more accustomed to our way of living here in Argentina, and we had started to claim that she belonged to us as she had lived her life with us.

Of all my friends, she was the most faithful, and losing her now I feel great loneliness. She used to collect my medication regularly – and that was not a small task.

When Stifin was in hospital, Mair would bring me food daily, and ensured that Stifin's nightclothes were clean, as I was personally unable to undertake that task.

On Thursdays, after I had lost Stifin, she would visit more often, and her pattern during these last years was to bring lunch already prepared for both of us. After we had eaten, she would take a siesta on a simple sofa. Then on to the prayer meeting, either in Edith's home or in Bethel chapel.

(2 January 2010)

Ada Lloyd Jones de Garavano, Puerto Madryn

A close friend since Mair's early days with the Methodists, Ada married a Methodist minister. Mair used to stay with them in their home in Puerto Madryn.

Mair came here on the last Monday of the month, and it was wonderful to see her and have an opportunity to share. After we had shared with each other and had renewed fellowship, I noticed that Mair would always bid us farewell with some wise word of advice – a word that would be a succour to my soul and a means of sustaining me when I faced difficult times. I miss her very much.

(4 January 2010)

Two remember the camps

Arié Lloyd de Lewis

Arié Lloyd de Lewis is a retired nursery teacher. A writer of prose and poetry, her special interest lies primarily in the history of women of the Chubut Valley.

I had a very high regard for Mair because she was a sister in the faith and in my heart. She was a dear friend and a faithful one, although we did not manage to meet as often as we would have liked. Indeed, I considered Mair to be one of the most faithful witnesses to the gospel that I have ever met during my lifetime.

I have happy memories of the time when Mair was working in the Methodist Church in Gaiman, where I lived, and contributed in a small way to the chapel's work.

I also have memories of the children's summer camp in Puerto Madryn. I remember that, although the weather was cold, many children came along after we'd been around the houses inviting them. Around a hundred children gathered. We were tired by the end of the day. We used to make all kinds of pictures because there were no photocopiers at that time. In the early hours of the morning, Mair would be busy preparing the pictures, whereas we could not resist yielding to sleep. The pictures would be ready in the morning but there's no knowing when Mair slept that night!

Mair had prepared a large bowl of rice pudding before setting off on our journey. There was much laughter as we tried to carry the dessert over such a distance in the lorry. Eating it at the end of the journey was a real treat.

We all clapped to congratulate Mair on having such a good idea.

Another memory I have is that of us boiling peaches and then counting the stones. We then played an innocent game of 'He loves me, he loves me not' with the children – one we really enjoyed. Mair made sure that the number of stones she provided meant, to our great delight, that our turn always ended with: 'He loves me.' How thoughtful of her.

Shortly after Mair's arrival in the Valley, I remember accompanying her and a company of young people on a trip to the seaside in the summer of 1965. This trip was part of the summer school camp arranged by the Methodist Church for all the churches of the denomination in Patagonia. The camp was held in a place called Belgrano Harbour beside the city of Bahiá Blanca in the province of Buenos Aires. This was Mair's first experience of a youth camp in this country.

Mair taught us a song. The words had to be simple because we were only six from the Chubut Valley who spoke Welsh. Here's a translation of the verse I remember to this day from the song:

> Jesus never fails,
> Jesus never fails,
> Heaven and earth shall pass away
> But Jesus never fails.
> *(Arthur Luther)*

And that was Mair's theme in our midst throughout the years, namely that Christ is alive for eternity.

I wrote a letter to St. David's Society some years ago to offer Mair's name as one who should be recognised for her work in spreading the Gospel in the community. (St.

David's Society gives this recognition every year to someone who has made a special contribution to the community on behalf of the Welsh language or culture.) Unfortunately, I was not successful and that is not surprising, given that the work of the Gospel, since the beginning of man's history, has been set to one side.

I can therefore testify that Mair's message has enriched many lives in the *Wladfa* through the Word of the Gospel, her example, and the Christian work that she fulfilled in the shop throughout the years.

Marlîn Ellis de Mellado

Lle Cul leads to the hills of Bryn Gwyn where the settlers fled during the floods. Marlîn Ellis de Mellado was raised on a farm there. Nowadays, Marlîn lives in Trelew.

The first memory I have of Mair is seeing her when I was a child in a prayer meeting in the Methodist Church, and then later her coming to our house to chat with my aunt Catherine (Catrin Ellis) for hours. We lived in the same house as my aunt, and I would be in my element listening to the discussion and learning about Mair's mission in our midst.

When Mair opened the shop in Trelew, I used to call on her and she was always so loving and affectionate towards me. In 1987, as I lived in Trelew by then, I began to attend Bible studies at Tabernacl chapel where Mair was recounting the history of Paul. I enjoyed those studies, and Mair became my friend, and I began to worship at Tabernacl from Sunday to Sunday.

Soon after this, my children went to the camps under the auspices of the Free Churches of the *Wladfa*. Mair was adamant that the camps should continue. That was when I agreed with two or three others to help Mair with organising everything, going round the shops comparing prices, as inflation was bad here at that time. We visited supermarkets. A menu was devised. Activities and trips were planned. And it is a fact that the leaders of the young people today, Graciela and Adrian for example, were the fruits of the early camps and the mark of the camps was upon them.

There was a difficult time for Mair when she lived in a caravan behind the vestry of Trelew chapel, until the women made a place for her to sleep in the vestry itself. The shop was moved in order to have more space. After all, her space in St. David's Hall was exceptionally small. The first move was to the front of the chapel, then came the shop directly opposite, which was an ideal location.

As President of the Union of Free Churches, Mair would ensure that those who came from Wales preached the Gospel, and this kept the churches active. Mair also used to emphasize that we needed to pray, and pray together, because unless a church prays, it will not grow. By praying together, she believed that we gave God greater glory, and as the suggestion of a raffle to raise funds to complete the new building for the minister was floated, Mair was of the view that there would be no blessing if we used that method of raising money.

Mair, therefore, was ready to stand up for a principle. As an example of this, in the Union Committee, she said she did not want to hear the members referring to the colour of the skin of the native people amongst them. She believed it was important not to be an unnecessary stumbling block to the indigenous people coming to the church. I have so many memories of her.

(March 2002)

102

Words from the Andes

Alwen Gilford Roberts, Esquel

A faithful member of Seion Chapel, Esquel, and
responsible for keeping the chapel's minutes.

Mair would stay with Ann Griffiths, Trevelin, when she
came to Cwm Hyfryd, later staying with us in Esquel. We
used to make enough food so that Mair could visit and
have dinner with us. Then a siesta would follow before
going to the evening service.

Mair was particularly thoughtful when I lost my first
little grand-daughter, Karen, in 1992. Karen had left
hospital, where she had been having medical help, to
'search for peace'. No one knew she had left her room.
She was lost for twenty days.

Mair arrived at nine o'clock on the morning of the last
day, having travelled by the night bus from Chubut
Valley where she lived. We had just learned that Karen's
body had been found, frozen, on the mountain. Realising
that I needed company, Mair stayed, and I will never
forget her kindness.

She was a balm to the open wounds of the Chubut
Valley and Cwm Hyfryd.

(March 2002)

Edith Wyn, Esquel

Freddie Green and Ann Griffiths's sister-in-law.

Mair, my husband Gwili's sister, was the first to meet
Mair in Bariloche, and then the Griffiths family met her.
I remember Mair in 1974 when we lived on the prairie in
an *estancia*, when we became great friends.

It involved considerable time and effort for Mair to come to work with us in Esquel and Trevelin, because it meant loosing two nights' sleep as the bus journey crossed the prairie during the night. At that time Mair stayed with us, and we used to talk about all manner of things till one o'clock in the morning, sharing experiences both happy and sad.

I used to enjoy the Welsh service in Seion, Esquel, and the four of us have been meeting to pray every month for years. Mair would join us when she was here, and was supportive of our efforts. As sisters in the Lord, used to praying together, we know that our future is in Christ.

(March 2002)

Mary Borda de Green, Trevelin

An English teacher who won the Chubut
Eisteddfod Chair in 2009, for a poem in memory of
her parents.

I first came to know Mair when I was in school in Bariloche where Mair arrived in 1964 to learn Spanish. When Mair, after five months, was allowed to visit the Welsh community here at the foot of the Andes, she stayed with Ann Griffiths and Mair Griffiths, my aunts in Troed-yr-Orsedd, Trevelin, and at my parents' home in Pennant.

Her chief contribution was helping us spiritually by explaining our Welsh connection to the faith. I often used to ask her during these last years, why she persisted in the work since the younger generation by now worship primarily in Spanish. Her answer was that she had been called to the work, even to the elderly. Indeed, her whole outlook emphasised that she was here to serve. We were extremely glad that she accepted a special Bible from the Bible Society as acknowledgement for her valuable work in the chapels and the Christian bookshop.

The returning
based on the poem 'Anatiomaros'
by T. Gwynn Jones

Anatiomaros . . .
Great of soul, matchless in virtue,
Crossed from the land of the ancients . . .
Mair, she of that winning radiance
And generous heart,
Yesterday returned
To that 'sun's paradise,
To the immortals'.
She crossed an ocean,
Exchanging old world for new,
Her Lord's servant true,
Nothing withholding.
She made of the vineyard
Assigned to her hand
A labour of love,
A care unceasing.
Hers a living sacrifice,
A life offered in service
Till finding her rest in the bosom
Of the One she adored.
Yesterday she crossed Jordan,
To the mansions prepared for her;
A table He'd spread for her.
Mair, she of that winning radiance
And generous heart,

Yesterday returned
To that 'sun's paradise,
To the immortals'.

MARY GREEN, Trevelin   *(October 2009)*

Translated by Phil Ellis

Meinir Evans, Trevelin

One of the descendants of Dalar Evans, and sister
to Iola Evans and Monw Hughes.

Mair would come and go, finally settling in the Chubut
Valley. She learned Spanish well – for that matter, she
did everything well. Mair was thoughtful and kind, and
when she came here at weekends she brought provisions
with her such as honey, butter, milk and a cake. I remember the window of her car freezing over at one time, and
Mair cleaning the window with a thermos of tea!

Mair would give back issues of the *Cylchgrawn
Efengylaidd* ('Evangelical Magazine') to me to read and
the Calendar every Christmas. After the shop had been
extended, many old books were kept in the library at the
back of the shop in Trelew. This library, like the shop, was
a precious resource.

(March 2002)

The Sunday School class
at Tabernacl chapel, Trelew

Interviews in March 2002.

May Williams de Hughes

A pianist and organist at Tabernacl for over
fifty years. A deaconess for over 20 years.

I have known Mair since she first came to the Valley. Her
unobtrusive way of working has been invaluable.

We have relied greatly on her to lead us and to lead
the chapels. If she is happy with a decision, we follow her
leading. Another fine characteristic is the way she
shares her fellowship with us and visits the sick.

The Sunday School has gone from strength to
strength. There were 84 present yesterday as we recom-
mence after the summer holidays. I remember a time
when there was only one little girl in the Sunday School,
and in the evening only five women. Mair persevered,
and the chapel remained open.

Indeed, the chapel is over a hundred years old – it is
the oldest building in Trelew. We inherited the building
from our fathers; now we are building a house for the
minister that will join us in due course. In the basement
of the building, there is space for the young people with
a hall, a small kitchen and bathroom. Then, above, there
is a home for the minister. We have been selling tea,
cakes, and shoes, and people have been giving gene-
rously. We've had amazing gifts, for example, 500 pesos
last Sunday from a woman who came here for a few days.
God wants us to finish the work.

Irvonwy (Monw) and Homer Hughes, Troad

Homer Hughes died in September 2009.

Monw

A deaconess at Tabernacl chapel, Trelew.

We were raised as children in the Andes. When it snowed, I remember we were unable to go to town for three months. So Sunday School would be in the home, and we have appreciated the upbringing we received. Dalar Evans was our grandfather's name.

I have known Mair since the very beginning, and remember her opening the service with prayer when she first came into our midst. I remember David Peregrine giving thanks for that intense prayer.

When there would be opposition at times to the evangelical message, Mair persevered and continued working. Indeed, Mair's presence changes the atmosphere. In committee work her dignity stands out.

After Homer and I had visited Wales, I remember asking Mair why she chose to live in the *Wladfa*. You see, I believe that Mair spent lonely years away from home, even though Mair's family have been over here to visit her. However, since she has had the car and the flat here in Trelew, her life has improved considerably. It has been a help to her family, when visiting, to see that Mair is in such a lovely place, and has made it easier for them to accept living without her.

My prayer, and Mair's prayer over the years, is to be seen in W. M. Hughes's book, *Ar Lannau'r Camwy* ('On the Banks of the Chubut'): 'Go forward as a hero to conquer, but in all your success do not forget to guard your own soul.'

Beryl Rowlands de Suárez, Trelew

A faithful member at Tabernacl chapel, Trelew.

Mair had a difficult time at the beginning. She was far from her family and country. I am thankful that she was strong in the faith and able to lean on her Lord.

Following the arrival of the first settlers, years of darkness were experienced. By today, things have begun to brighten, and certainly Mair has been an instrument in enabling the Gospel to shine.

In the 1980s, I suffered from depression, and Violeta Brooks invited me back to Tabernacl. Mair was leading the Sunday School, and going there was beneficial for me. We received much blessing, and Mair and the members were so pleased to see me. Later we decided to meet on Thursdays with Mair. She began to teach us from the little book *Y Ffordd i'r Bywyd* ('The Way to Life'). That's how I came to believe, and was moved from darkness to light. I had not understood that we were all sinners. I am grateful for such peace and happiness. I felt a desire then to throw open the window to proclaim to others what had happened. When Gweneira retired as the small children's Sunday School teacher, I was asked to take them, and that's what I did.

I am grateful also for Carwyn Arthur's contribution when he ministered here in August 1990. He was 26 years of age at the time, and he began to speak of the Revival that had taken place in the Valley. He showed that there was much need of repentance for what followed, namely the history of the churches and the division that followed. He emphasised the need for us to pray for a further awakening.

So I began to appreciate the opportunity I had to pray

in the early morning as my husband worked in Rawson. When I suggested to the Sunday School class the idea of meeting together, there was silence. But when we were outside, Mair came up quietly to tell me that she would be happy to join with me. Therefore, in the mornings, between 7.30 and 8.30, I would visit Mair's home to pray. This was our routine for years.

Then we began to meet for prayer in the chapel, and by now we have prayed together for eleven years. This was an opportunity to practise the language and was a great blessing to me. This is also good for the Lord's work here in the Valley as we are seeing growth. Claudia, who grew up here at Tabernacl, is now with us. After being away studying, she is now back to lead us. We see a good congregation coming together in the Sunday School. The Lord is blessing, and I trust that we will not grieve him.

Eileen James de Jones and Dewi Mefin Jones, Trelew

Eileen is a former English teacher and
Dewi Mefin is a prominent member of the
Wladfa Gorsedd.

A non-denominational spirit characterises the chapels of the Valley. There is a willingness to worship together, at Tabernacl, Bethesda, Bethel and Bryn Crwn. And our story? Well, my family and I worshipped in Bethesda, and Dewi Mefin, my husband, worshipped at Bryn Crwn. It was not difficult for us to cross the fence! The original Bryn Crwn chapel was swept away by floods, and some Baptists, Calvinistic Methodists and Independents decided to build a non-denominational chapel after all that destruction. So the present chapel at Bryn Crwn came into being. Consequently, as a child that used to worship in Bryn Crwn, Dewi did not know what a denomination was.

Few meet now in the services in the Valley, so we gather once a month in Bryn Crwn, and once a month in Bethesda, alternately. Also a Sunday School for children began some years ago, and the children come to be taught. Then, in the Spanish language meetings Mair conducts, the children come to the service and worship with us.

We regard Mair as one of us, as she has been with us for so many years. She has become familiar with the place. Her selfless presence here has been very precious indeed. She came here at a time when seeing someone from Wales was very unusual. As we are now the fourth generation, there are many mixed marriages, and we succeed in co-existing with people of all nationalities.

Mair, therefore, is one of our people, and it is to her we turn for advice, and her contribution in our midst is outstanding. Mair is here, and that's what really counts.

Mary Ann Rogers

A member of Nasareth chapel, Drofa Dulog, and of the Sunday School at Tabernacl chapel.

Having Mair with us has been a great benefit. I have often been surprised that she has been able to leave her family for so long. We find it strange when Mair is not here. When Mair returns to Wales for two to three months, she is drawn back to us, here in the *Wladfa*.

Elena Davies de Arnold, Trelew

I remember Mair when she was very young, and I appreciated her warm personality. She has devoted her life to the *Wladfa,* and both of us have been great friends; we were like 'night owls' enjoying conversation for hours about *y pethe* (the values and traditions that are associated with Welsh life at its best). We would read a great deal and use the old books that belonged to my father-in-law – detailed commentaries.

I would be given the responsibility for the Sunday School class when Mair returned to Wales, aiming to hold the class's interest by keeping them involved while she was so far away.

Mair is very wise, because it's not always easy to live in such a small community. We are a small group. But Mair has succeeded in living her Christian life blameless in the sight of everyone, wisely keeping her own counsel. For that reason, she is admired by all – both the Welsh and the Spanish.

(March 2002)

Raquel Hawys Davies, Trelew

Hawys is a former nurse and is one of those who
show visitors round Tabernacl chapel.

I am one of six children, and we were raised in Drofa Dulog. The first chapel in Drofa Dulog was close to the river. In 1932, when I was six years of age, the flood came and I remember having to escape to the rocks.

Many people from Buenos Aires visit Tabernacl chapel. Mair encouraged and prepared me for the challenge of welcoming these visitors. She explained to me that Welsh is a very old and unique language. The inhabitants of the North consider Trelew a miracle, with its plain, simple and beautiful chapels, so different from the grand churches of the Catholics.

Mair helped us through difficult experiences and has kept us from becoming bitter. She was everything to us.

(23 December 2009)

Virma Griffiths de Hudson

I used to talk frequently with Mair as she was a great help to me. She used to call me 'Virma *fach*', and she used to sympathise with me because of my difficult background. I would accompany Mair in the car, sharing with her sometimes while travelling to chapels in the Valley, where she would officiate.

She gave me a Welsh Bible as a gift six years ago, and I was able to study the Word with her in the shop. I learned a great deal, and it's so hard to go to Tabernacl now without seeing Mair, who was everything in the chapel. She always had a smile, and her face shone.

Mair worked year after year by coming and going, coming and going. The whole Valley will miss her.

(5 January 2010)

Martin and Charlotte Jacobson,
Bryn Gwyn College

Leaders of the Patagonian Bible Institute, near Gaiman.

In 1984, when we arrived in the Valley as missionaries from Kentucky, we met Mair as we also lived in Trelew. It was she who led us around Tabernacl chapel and spoke clearly and memorably about the history of the first company of settlers who came to the Valley. Her words remained very clear in our minds. Another early memory we have is of her playing the harmonium in Bryn Crwn chapel.

Then, when this Bible College began in Bryn Gwyn, Mair gave us a china tea set so that we could welcome visitors properly. Also we remember her helping a student called Veronica (who attended this Bible College) with her school studies. That student went on to be a missionary in the jungle in Peru.

What characterized Mair was her deep hunger for God. We admit that it is very easy in church and Christian work not to continue to grow personally. And this is where being taught by Christians from different traditions and backgrounds has been a valuable education to us. We appreciate, for example, the story of Rees Howells, *Intercessor! Welsh Warrior*.

Shortly after we arrived in the Valley, Tegai Roberts showed us a letter by a missionary to Seion chapel, nearby, saying he was indebted to the education and training he had received in the Sunday School there. As we were eager to understand more about the Welsh and their background, Mair agreed to translate for us letters from Robert Owen Jones's book, *Yr Efengyl yn y Wladfa*.

This was a great help in enabling us to appreciate the heroism of the early years.

In our tradition, retreats are important, and Mair enjoyed coming to share fellowship with us when her timetable allowed. She appreciated the opportunity to sit under other ministries. After a while, Mair asked if she might conduct the camps of the Union of Free Churches here, and that's what happened.

There is an open spirit here in Patagonia to receive the good news of Jesus Christ. And, as Providence would have it, much of this is due to the work of the early pioneers. God has given us indeed the privilege of following in the footsteps of the early pioneers who paid such a high price, and Mair was indeed part of that succession.

At Mair's funeral what created the greatest impression upon us were the words of Delfín Viano, who spoke of Mair's work in selling more than 50,000 Bibles on behalf of the *Association da Biblica*, not forgetting all the other Bibles sold through the shop. Another speaker concluded her contribution by saying that Mair had lived her life amongst us as a true Christian. We were moved by her words.

From the perspective of our ministry, we have been praying over the years for more teaching, for those who come to believe, on discipleship. We have seen a great number in South America becoming Christians, but have been disappointed by their lack of commitment to live the Christian faith from day to day. There is a substantial emphasis here in the College on teaching such aspects to students as part of the training programme for residents.

Losing Mair Davies is a great loss. We are grateful for having known her.

(*1 January 2010*)

115

Three tributes given at
the funeral of Mair Davies
24 August 2009

Observations by Judith Hughes de Torres

Miss Mair has left us to enter the presence of the Lord.

I knew her from my childhood, but it was not until the mid 1990s that I came to know her well. I remember three situations that brought me closer to her.

Firstly, in the work of the Union of Free Churches, when Mair was president between 1999 and 2003. Characteristically, she took her work seriously by seeking the Lord's leading and respecting his will. At all times she endeavoured to please her God. She aimed to ensure that God's word was being taught in every Welsh chapel. Among her last projects was the publication of the bilingual New Testament in Welsh and Spanish.

Secondly, in the reception class for new members, where she directed us in love and complete commitment. For her, every Bible lesson was to be considered as a challenge to our lives, and she communicated this to us. Mair was sensitive to God's voice, and at all times gave glory to the Lord.

Then, thirdly, her fondness for children and young people kept her fully occupied, ever mindful of their needs, and instrumental in the activities organised in the chapel. She was alive to the plight of others, and always ready to participate and help.

Mair was always good company, a loyal and helpful companion. With her pleasant and thoughtful nature she always had the right word at the right time. You could always rely on her.

Miss Mair taught and lived the Christian life.

May Hughes, Trelew, read a tribute by Mair's family.
Here is that tribute:

It is a great privilege to pay tribute, from far-off Wales, to our dear sister Mair. It was a terrible shock to hear on Thursday morning, 20 August, from Carwyn and Alicia, that she was ill in hospital in Trelew, and then a few hours later, that she had died and left us so suddenly.

With a heavy heart, therefore, we seek to extend this tribute to her, realising that no words can adequately express Mair's worth to us.

She was born in a little village outside Lampeter called Cwm-ann – the third of eight children – before moving to a small farm called Bercoed Ganol in Cardiganshire. She enjoyed farm work and would have made an excellent farm wife had she not set her eyes on a higher calling.

She received a great deal of kindness from the people of the *Wladfa* from the outset, and she always spoke very warmly of them. Her letters would be full of the activities of her close and obliging friends, who helped her from day to day, and woe betide anyone who said anything bad about the *Wladfa*!

117

She spoke often of the people of Gaiman, Dolavon, Trelew, Bryn Crwn, Bryn Gwyn and Esquel, and we became familiar with enchanting names such as Drofa Dulog, Tir Halen, Dyffryn yr Allorau and Gorsedd y Cwmwl.

Naturally, she was homesick for her family and her birthplace, at first, but the *Wladfa* won her heart entirely, and that's where she wanted to be to the end. And she had her wish.

We remember her returning to us full of enthusiasm about the beauty of some districts in Patagonia, and eager for us to come over to see for ourselves and meet the amiable people who had won her heart. She loved the people of Patagonia sincerely and she was in her element amongst them.

Our homes are full of the little presents Mair bought back to us and the children over the years: a dainty little model of Tabernacl chapel, urging us to remember Patagonia every time we dusted it; little footballs on which we could hang our keys from the time of the World Cup; little dainty arrows that became tie-pins or were placed on necklaces – all very distinctive and a ready talking-point.

The nephews and nieces would be delighted if Aunty Mair could stay with them, because she was so patient and would tell a story – and she never scolded them! Many was the time when a tasty cake would be awaiting them when they got home from school.

It was very strange to hear Mair, in the early years, talking of celebrating Christmas in broad sunlight on a beach, and us unable to imagine such a thing. Mair's greatest happiness, as you know, was sharing the Gospel, helping in the chapels, and selling Bibles in the Christian bookshops.

Without naming names, we would like to thank you, as a family, from the heart, for the way you accepted Mair into your hearts and for the help and support given to her efforts over the years. Also for the warm welcome we all received on our journeys to the *Wladfa* from time to time – we then understood why she was so fond of you all.

Naturally the loss of Mair has caused us much grief, but she has now arrived home and seen the face of her Saviour, her faith changed into sight. It is a sadness to us as a family that we cannot be present on the particular day of farewell to our beloved Mair in Gaiman, but our hearts will be with you as you sing her favourite hymns in memory of her. Her many friends here in Wales will join in your mourning and loss, and are grateful to God for the life and service of Mair for almost half a century.

When Mair's two nieces, Sara and Luned, come to the *Wladfa* in December, they will not have the pleasure of her company as intended, but there will be an opportunity to place flowers on her grave on behalf of us all.

(Y Drafod, Spring 2010)

119

Carlos Ruiz and his wife Marcela

Carlos is one of the children of the Valley who has
returned to succeed Mair, in the work through the
medium of Spanish, in the Chubut Valley. His wife,
Marcela, is a Crafts and Design teacher in Trelew.
They have three daughters, Julieta, Lucia and
Gisel. Here is a translation of Carlos's observations
in Spanish.

I refer to Ephesians 4. God gave gifts to the church and
Mair was a gift. In Luke 10:38–42 we have the story of
Martha and Mary. Mary chose the better part, she was at
the feet of Jesus. Mair Davies also sought His Word, and
prayed for revival in the chapels. She was a spiritual
reference point. In Jeremiah 29:10 we have the words:

' . . . I will come to you and do for you all the good
things I have promised.'

Indeed, I believe that there is here a promise that the
word that Mair has sown will awaken in the hearts of
those who have heard.

On a personal note, Mair was one who walked with
me; now I must learn to walk alone. We had many plans,
but Mair has gone before they materialised. I must go on
without her. Mair taught me to love the Welsh chapels, to
see them with new eyes. If the word is drowsy in our
hearts, let us pray that it will be awakened.

Examples, in translation, of Mair Davies's work from *Y Drafod / El Mentor*

Hats

One thing I regret as I cast an eye over the interesting years I've had the privilege of enjoying in the *Wladfa* is that I did not keep a detailed diary from the very first.

As memory is such a fragile thing, with the passage of time, many valuable experiences have disappeared, to return no more. But one of the earliest memories that remains is being present at a preaching service in Carmel chapel, Dolavon, and sharing the service with the Reverend D. J. Peregrine. I cannot remember the occasion in detail, but I do remember that the chapel was full.

My sister, Myfanwy, had given me a special gift before I set off for the *Wladfa*, that is, a smart hat, chestnut or brick colour – made of felt and smooth to the touch. I know she paid a good price for it! The hat appeared at the special meeting in Dolavon, and this was one of the rare occasions I believe it had an outing.

The custom of wearing hats was rapidly dying out in the *Wladfa*, especially amongst the younger generation, and I was myself at that time one of that generation. And although I had made a particular effort to carry about a dozen hats with me from Wales, they had a short life.

Most of them finished their days in summer camps for young people in some sketch or other, since Pastor Perrin was in his element at that time presenting sketches, and hats were a particular attraction.

To return to Dolavon, after the meeting I was invited to supper at Treborth, the home of Mr and Mrs Richard James in Bethesda. I had newly returned from Wales, where it was usual to eat a light supper. As a result their supper, with beef and potatoes, was nothing less than a feast. And I remember that the evening had been enjoyable with some teasing, as you can imagine, on the part of Richard James, and Mr Peregrine responding with his quiet, subtle humour.

It is a pity that many of the values that, at one time, characterised us as Welsh people are in danger of being lost in our days – the close-knit community, with its high standards, keeping one's word, full chapels and a living faith. Yes, and why not, smart hats!

(Y Drafod 2000)

A Poem for Recitation

Home

But a roof, four walls, some windows, a door,
Yet did anywhere's name ever come to mean more?

That tenderest care, that love, that refrain,
That fire-side closeness, that shared joy and pain.

What learning from college or school could compare
With heart-lessons lovingly taught us there?

This haven of respite from wearisome strife,
Was part of God's purpose when first He formed life.

May heav'n's blessing rest on such homes far and near,
May God keep and protect from all peril and fear.

(Couplets recited by Gweneira Davies de Quevedo.
Translated by Phil Ellis)

A tribute

(to Gerallt Williams, Bod Iwan)

The Lord Jesus told one of his fellow-countrymen once, 'Behold, an Israelite, indeed, in whom there is no guile,' and I cannot help thinking that Jesus could have spoken these words to describe our friend and brother, Gerallt Williams. He was a sincere person, upright, noble, honest with a good heart, ready to oblige and was greatly respected throughout the community.

We remember him competing in the eisteddfodau, and for years as the Keeper of the Sword, asking with dignity, 'Is there peace?'

We remember him conducting innumerable funerals in the Upper Valley.

We know that it was for his help that the farmers of the neighbourhood would call when they feared losing an animal.

The chapel occupied a central place in his life. Bryn Crwn was his chapel. He had spent his childhood there, but Gerallt was open-minded enough to enter any place of worship in the Valley to attend services and give support. His faith was sincere. He was honest and open enough to ask the minister at the end of a service whether his faith was of the right kind. He wanted to be sure.

I have heard some saying how they liked to listen to Gerallt taking part in a meeting – the way he read the Word of God slowly and sensitively with his singing enriching the praise also. He had a strong bass voice and was never happier than when he sang.

I remember well the journey, about 1980, to the waterfalls of Iguazu with Mariana and Gerallt in a Ford vehicle. We had taken the *Caniedydd* and *Cantico Nuevo* (New Songs) with us, and we travelled miles, singing one hymn after the other with Mariana all the while knitting and praising our efforts!

Despite our loss, we are thankful that he did not suffer long, and his wife, Silvia, testifies that he was a long-suffering and uncomplaining patient. He left us, as he had lived, peacefully and without fuss.

Without a doubt, the *Wladfa* is a poorer place now that Gerallt has gone.

(Y Drafod, Autumn 2009)

Moriah

       Meeting place of our dear fathers,
       Once blessed with heaven's presence nigh.
1880   Resolute, its doors still opened   1980
       If gale blew fierce or flood rose high.
       Again resound, sweet Gospel message,
       Here may many heed its cry.

(Y Drafod, Spring 1980. Translated by Phil Ellis)

A hymn

(Tune: *Lausanne*)

So much hast Thou wrought, sweet Jesus,
For a sinner such as me,
Laying down Thy life as ransom
There on Calv'ry's cruel tree.

God Himself knew death for my sake –
God Himself in human span;
O! that gracious plan eternal,
Reuniting God and man.

Why such kindness, long I ponder,
Lavished on an impure heart?
Love stands as the only reason:
Love o'erflows, all love Thou art.

How can ever I re-pay Thee
For such mercy freely shown?
Only my heart-felt repentance
May I offer at Thy throne.

As I seek Thy gracious presence,
Let love's ardour never cease,
Each day spent in serving brightened
By the beauty of Thy peace.

Then, Thy radiant glory viewing,
Endless hymns of praise begun,
Worthier worship I will bring Thee:
Glorious Saviour, God's own Son.

*(The winning entry in the hymn-writing competition in
the Trelew Eisteddfod, 1993. Translated by Phil Ellis)*